For UK orders: please contact Bookpoint Ltd, 130 Milton Park, Abingdon, Oxon OX14 4SB. Telephone: +44 (0) 1235 827720. Fax: +44 (0) 1235 400454. Lines are open 09.00–18.00, Monday to Saturday, with a 24-hour message answering service. You can also order through our website www.madaboutbooks.co.uk

British Library Cataloguing in Publication Data A catalogue record for this title is available from The British Library.

Library of Congress Catalog Card Number: On file.

This edition, first published in UK 2003 by Hodder Headline Plc, 338 Euston Road, London NW1 3BH

Typeset by Servis Filmsetting Ltd, Manchester, England
Printed in Great Britain for Hodder & Stoughton Educational, a Division of Hodder Headline Plc, 338 Euston Road, London NW1 3BH by Cox & Wyman Ltd, Reading, Berkshire.

Impression number   10 9 8 7 6 5 4 3 2 1
Year   2007 2006 2005 2004 2003

Contents

Series Introduction

Perhaps you have had an idea, or wanted to achieve something, but known that you not only need some skills but also help with taking the risk and doing it for real. Maybe you have thought 'it is easy for him/her but not for me . . .'

This series is written for people who haven't got the time (or money) to attend a long training course or who are not lucky enough to be managed and mentored by a star in the field in which they want to succeed. These books will be 'back pocket' resources that will inspire and give practical tips that you can read up on and use in the next few minutes. They will also help you feel confident in taking skills that you already have into new situations at work, home and the community.

Lesley Gosling
Q. Learning

Introduction: Consultant

If you are a consultant in any field, working for any size of organization, from the massive to the one man plus the dog, then this book is for you!

You may not even call yourself a consultant. For example, you might be an engineer – civil or software – the key point is that you offer your technical expertise to a client – that is our definition of a consultant.

The aim of this book is to help you to become the very best consultant in your field by building up your client facing skills, and by showing you how vital these are. In some ways, this is more important than your technical expertise. If you find that surprising, read on – this is definitely the book for you!

Anna Hipkiss has had extensive experience of consulting across a number of fields, and she has been both an internal and an external consultant, and an employer of both! Unusually, Anna's career spans several disciplines – HR, Marketing and IT Services Management, which eventually led her into General Management as a Director in an IT company in the finance sector. Before that, she had worked in the engineering, consumer products and IT industries. She has employed numerous consultants in all these fields as external suppliers, and has worked with many internal consultants. She has also worked herself as an external HR consultant, and as an internal Marketing consultant. In her role as IT Services Director, she ran a division which included 150 software consultants (all permanent employees), so she really has approached the subject from every angle!

Apart from her breadth and depth of experience, she also brings to the subject a fresh approach, firmly anchored in the real world, which offers practical material which you can put to immediate use to help you become your best and beyond!

Preface

This book started from my e-learning program: 'The Consultant's Guide to Consulting' (see 'References', page 245), and it has been interesting to discover how differently the two media are composed. In a book you have the luxury of words, which are used sparingly on screen; in a program you have more scope for interaction. I believe that I have now produced two pieces of learning, which are quite different, but complementary, and they can be used in tandem or in sequence.

It has been a delight to meet so many consultants, and to have room in the book to quote them extensively. Irene Nathan from Interpersonal Relations Group made the comment that, 'I often consult other consultants on different subjects, as part of my learning process. I believe you need to keep yourself fresh and alive and learned and knowledgeable – that is the most important thing you can offer, whatever your subject.'

This illustrates a major theme of the book – the consultant's love of self-development. I have really enjoyed having this personal opportunity to consult so many people, which I can share with you now.

Acknowledgements

I have consulted many consultants and employers of consultants in writing this book and I would like to thank them all for their very rich contribution, in particular:

Sir John Harvey Jones, Mary Ahmad – Corporate HR Partners, Mark Brown – Innovation Centre Europe, Sue Goble – Siebel Systems UK Ltd, Vic Hartley – Vertex Consultants, Mary Hill – Pecaso UK Ltd, Peter Honey – Peter Honey Learning, Gill Hunt – Skillfair, Steven Hunt – MWH, Frank Milton – Price Waterhouse Coopers, David Mitchell – Oracle UK Ltd, Irene Nathan – Interpersonal Relations Group, Leon Sadler – SAP UK Ltd, Janet Simmons – Pecasco UK Ltd, Penny Stocks – Cap Gemini Ernst & Young UK.

Finally, I would like to thank my husband Richard, for his unfailing support, and Lesley Gosling for her inspiring vision!

DISCLAIMER

I have gone to great lengths to use real case study material in this book and I have gone to similar lengths to disguise the companies and the people involved, to protect everyone's confidentiality. If, in creating these disguises, I have used names which you recognize, this is unfortunate, because, as they say at the beginning of all the best books, all the names I have used are fictional. Any resemblance to real people or companies is purely coincidental.

CHAPTER 1

What if . . . ?

The roots of true achievement lie in the will to become the best that you can become.

HAROLD TAYLOR

Seize opportunity by the beard, for it is bald behind.

BULGARIAN PROVERB

- ℚ **What if every consulting project I did counted as a stunning success?**
- ℚ **What if all my clients were perfectly reasonable and a pleasure to deal with?**
- ℚ **What if business just flowed in my direction, with no effort at all?**

This book is about helping you to make those dreams come true. You may be a seasoned professional, or new to this field. You may be employed by one of the major consultants, or you may work alone from an office in your spare room. The aim of this book is to help you on your way to achieving greater success as a consultant.

WHY THIS BOOK IS DIFFERENT

This book is different from other books you may read on the subject. Apart from offering you plenty of 'real meat' or serious content, in the way that most books offer you things on a plate, it also provides you with a knife and fork, and an appetite, which is what you will find in the early chapters. You may feel that you already have these, but it is worth checking. They will make the difference between just reading a useful book, and actually doing something with what you have learned.

Thinking inside and outside the box

What you will get on your plate is plenty of sensible, inside the box thinking, spiced with lots of practical experience. The way we help you to develop your appetite, and the tools we give you to consume what is on that plate, are generally outside the box ideas.

Getting inspiration

When you embark on a road that is new to you but well trodden by others, it is very helpful to have a role model to inspire you. Someone you can relate to, whose footsteps you feel capable of following. We have therefore included a number of potential role models for you to choose from, and details of the road they followed to success. You should work on the principle that if they can do it, so can you! You may not believe this 100 per cent, but if you take on the belief temporarily and act as if it were true, this opens up your mind and your options for achieving success.

Sources of learning

The learning in this book will come from three sources. First of all from you, as we help you to unpick your own magic and apply it in different ways to different situations. It is easy to underrate your own skills. Have you noticed that people admire a skill in you that you simply take for granted? We will examine how to transfer that skill and broaden its use.

The second source of learning will be from studying the experts, the special group of consultants we have chosen as models for success. These are prominent figures in their different fields, who have a track record we want to emulate, and skills we want to analyse and use.

The third source of learning will be from all the real life case studies, which are woven into the book, not just from experts, but from many different sources. They are, of necessity, anonymous in order to honour that key commitment of any consultant to protect client confidentiality, but they are no less real for that, and provide solid experience that we can learn from. Often these examples cover what went wrong, as well as what went right, so that you can learn from others' mistakes as well as their expertise.

When you have absorbed all three sources of learning, we will challenge you to be creative in applying ideas in new ways, to enable you to capture and develop the difference that makes the difference – to deliver greater success to you as a consultant in whatever way you choose to define it.

USING THIS BOOK IF YOU ARE A CORPORATE CONSULTANT

This book is written with you in mind. It generally takes the viewpoint of a consultant who is part of a project team, often based on a client site. It deals with the problems that a consultant faces internally within his or her own organization, as well as externally with the client: the manager who is never there when you need them; the colleagues who let you down; the training that you miss; the conflict between loyalty to your distant company, and to your good friend the client; the recognition and career progression that you do not get when you are hidden away on some remote site. If these issues sound familiar to you, then read on because the book contains much experience and potential learning on these subjects.

Because many consultants, unlike you, are self-employed, with some very different concerns, there is a chapter on setting up your own business. It contains several case studies, including people who have moved from being an employed consultant to setting up on their own. You may find it useful to understand this perspective, if only to confirm that this is not a career route for you!

USING THIS BOOK IF YOU ARE A SELF-EMPLOYED CONSULTANT

This book has much to offer you! The skills of a successful consultant do not change with your employment status. However, you also need skills in running a business, such as finance and marketing. In Chapter 16 you will find information on marketing your services. Chapter 17 covers the basic elements of setting up and running an independent business.

Some of the material in this book refers to the consultant as part of a project team, and suggests that you refer to your manager for advice. You may often work alone with the client, and certainly will not have a manager to refer to. However, you will often be part of a client team, even if that is not specifically your brief, and it is important to take team considerations into account. Similarly, you may work as part of a provider project team, in which case, although you are not an employee, you will certainly be acting as part of that provider's organization, and will have a project manager to refer to.

When you are working alone and you hit a real problem, instead of taking advice from your non-existent manager, think of a mentor or a friend who could be a sounding board for you and perform much the same function as a manager. Many lone consultants have very useful reciprocal relationships, where they offer each other advice and support – a kind of 'buddy' system is very useful to cultivate. So when you see the words 'Consult your manager', think in terms of a helpful colleague.

The thinking behind this book

Much of the content of this book is built on years of practical consulting experience, and the perspectives of many different people. This will take you a long way on the road to success.

It is also helpful to adopt a way of thinking that opens your mind to new perspectives and enables you to see how you might find the difference that makes the difference for you. To think in this new way, you simply adopt some new beliefs, such as 'There is a solution to every problem.'

You may believe this already, or you may refuse to accept that a nice solution is sitting round every corner. That is a very normal response, so please just try the belief on for size, and see how it feels, knowing you can take it off again. Doing this is the equivalent of adopting a presupposition – something that you do not have to permanently accept, but which you hold for the time it is useful to you.

Now presuppose that there is a solution to every problem while you are reading this book and seeking to find ways of becoming more successful as a consultant. Experience how enabling it will be, if you can hold that belief for this period. If you can do that, you are ready for the whole list.

These are the presuppositions that you will find useful to hold while you are becoming a more successful consultant.

- **There is a solution to every problem.**

- **The map is not the territory.** This means that the way you see things – your map – is not the same as anyone else's. Everybody sees life in different ways, even though they think they are seeing the same thing! This is a vital presupposition when managing a client relationship.

- **The meaning of communication is in the response you get.** In other words, what you intended to say is irrelevant; it is what the person hears that matters. A man might say to his wife 'Is it time for lunch?' She might hear, 'Lunch is late, you are failing in your domestic duties, and are therefore less loveable.' The husband might be amazed by that, when all he was really doing was checking the timing of a meal!

- **There is no failure, only feedback.** This is a very constructive way of looking at life. Learning usually involves making mistakes of some kind and those mistakes are usually a vital part of the learning process. Sometimes it takes many attempts before you get it right. In a learning environment, such as a training course, this is considered normal; in the 'real world' it is often viewed as unacceptable. Obviously you make every effort to avoid failure, but when it happens treat it as a source of learning, and you will progress further and faster towards success.

🍃 **If someone else can do something, so can you.** This is linked to another presupposition: **Everyone already has everything they need to achieve what they want.** If you can believe both of these things on a temporary basis, it will enable you to do so much more. You are almost certainly going to say that an unfit 40-year-old could never become an Olympic athlete, and of course there are going to be some physical limitations, but they do not generally apply to becoming a consultant, do they?

🍃 **The person with the most flexibility in thinking and behaviour has the most influence in any interaction.** This is a vital presupposition, and underlies most of the teaching on negotiation and influencing skills. An overt exercise of power, unless taken to extremes, will not necessarily win the battle against the flexible thinker.

🍃 **If you always do what you always did, you will always get what you always got.** The fact that you are reading this book suggests that you want to do things differently, and adopting all these presuppositions is a great place to start.

Progress now

Go through each of the presuppositions, and test whether you can take it on while you are learning. If you find a particular presupposition difficult, ask what is stopping you from taking it on temporarily. Then imagine what it would be like if you could . . . What would you be able to do differently?

Let's look at an example. Kay hates giving presentations. Her boss, Nigel, is a brilliant public speaker, witty and fluent, and just being with him makes her feel more inadequate. When she thinks about the presupposition 'If someone else can do something, so can you,' she thinks of Nigel and dismisses it. Just the thought of him stops her taking it on.

Now she forces herself to imagine that she does believe she can do public speaking – she cannot quite make the stretch to Nigel, who seems at Olympic standard compared to her, but she can imagine being competent, perhaps very competent. As she imagines, she starts to think about what she needs to do to get her to that comfortable level of competence. The presupposition is enabling her to move forward on a path towards success.

Take each presupposition in turn and test it out. If it is difficult, do what Kay did: focus on what stops you, then go beyond it.

In this same context, think of people you know who, in your view, are good consultants. Imagine what specific advice they might give you to enable you to hold these presuppositions, and to take you forward on the road to success.

CHAPTER 2

Consulting Excellence at Work

The way to do is to be.

ANON

Our greatest glory is not in never falling, but in rising every time we fall.

CONFUCIUS

Throughout this book there are contributions from consultants in many different fields, at different stages of their career: all very successful, all potential role models.

THE CORPORATE CONSULTANT

In this chapter we will examine some career success stories, so that you can take a look at what people have achieved, and how they have achieved it. These are all consultants working for large organizations, so you will see how they have risen up the organizational ladder. Apart from describing their career, they also have valuable insights into aspects of the role of a consultant, which reinforce many of the messages in this book.

THREE SUCCESS STORIES

Similarly, in the chapter on starting your own business, we profile consultants who have been successful independently, and again include valuable insights into the consulting role.

PENNY STOCKS

Vice President, Cap Gemini Ernst & Young

PS: Consulting is very hard work, and not nearly as glamorous as people think. Projects happen in Crewe, Glasgow and Liverpool, not always in Paris and Rome, as people like to imagine. And when you do go to Paris, you only see an office and the airport! At 4 o'clock in the morning when the photocopier has stopped working and you have a presentation to deliver at 8 a.m., you discover what real hard work means.

Despite these comments, Penny clearly loves consulting, and she tells how she came to be Vice President of a very large organization in her mid thirties.

PS: I studied management sciences at Manchester University in the early 1980s. I joined Rover cars as a graduate trainee in HR. I started in the field of Industrial Relations, but I found it to be all talk and no action, so I moved into HR more broadly and worked in three very different departments, gaining experience particularly in managing change. Then I was approached by Price Waterhouse, and I became a consultant, learning the basics of the profession, which I would describe as really understanding the client's problems, scoping the work accurately, and then delivering a high quality product. In those days a sale worth £20,000 merited a bottle of champagne. Today, a sale would need to exceed a million before we celebrate.

The core of my work was around helping people make the journey into change, and that was very difficult to sell, because it is so intangible. I therefore set about translating jargon into tangible and practical things that clients will buy.

After seven successful years I started to run out of space and so I joined Ernst & Young, who were just struggling with the concept of framing their people offering, and so this was the perfect opportunity for me. I joined as a Managing Consultant with a staff of five, which I grew to 30, eventually becoming Vice President. Through the merger with Cap Gemini the team grew to 60. Our role to date has been to help clients manage the people part of organizational change. A new software system, or the outsourcing of – say – the finance function: all of these changes have major people implications.

AH: What is the secret of your success?

PS:

💧 You need to have a belief in what you want to do.

 Q You take risks. You are prepared to put your neck above the parapet and stand out amongst your peers.

Q You focus on doing an excellent delivery job, and building a good track record.

Q You find good mentors. Some you just take to, others you seek out and develop the relationship.

Q You become a leader amongst your peers. You develop your own brand, and then just deliver.

AH: What is your brand now?

PS: My brand is being able to put forward successful and practical ways to help people change as part of major transformation projects.

AH: What are your major learning points as a consultant?

PS: Agree with a client exactly what they are expecting. Both the deliverable and the way you will work with them. It is in this area that most litigation takes place, so it cannot be agreed at too granular a level – almost down to storyboards of the project.

Be very clear on who the client is – who is paying the bill. It can often happen that the project sponsor is not your most frequent contact. Sometimes consultants are hired over the head of the person you deal with day to day. Sometimes that person may feel threatened or alienated and may not wish to cooperate with you. It is vital to maintain your link with the sponsor in this situation.

Take time to listen to the client and to really understand what the issue is. Do not produce your standard solution and then try cutting and pasting to make it fit.

AH: What makes a good consultant?

PS: It really helps if people have done a proper job. Consulting isn't a proper job, it's too much fun! Seriously, particularly in the change management field, it makes it a lot easier to look a client across the table and be firm by having been out there yourself. It may be different in the technical areas. (In effect, the company does hire graduates into other disciplines.) Clients are getting more sophisticated. They are no longer satisfied with the people who have read the books. They want consultants who have a lot of knowledge and experience and can give practical guidance and advice.

I also look for exceptional communication skills, the ability to listen, understand and form a view very swiftly. The person must very quickly have presence when meeting clients, and not be fearful of walking into difficult situations. There will be times when things won't work with the client, and they need to have the inner strength to take the knocks and move on. Few clients tell you that you have done a good job, so you need confidence and a belief in yourself.

Finally I want a really good team player, and lots of enthusiasm.

AH: What are the worst sins a consultant can commit?

PS:

1 Arrogance. Not listening. Already knowing the answer.

2 Complaining and moaning about the client internally, but in a public place. Confidentiality is a fundamental commitment to the client, and you never know who's listening. If the client has weaknesses, they have asked for your help, so you should respect that.

3 Taking the Big Company approach: 'We are the great ABC . . . consultants, and we will do it **to** you, not **with** you.'

4 Finally there's the opposite of arrogance, not being challenging enough to the client. Giving them what they want and not what they need.

Penny's honest and open approach to what she does clearly wins the trust of her clients, and delivers more business. This is also her approach with her own team, where a priority for her is to generate a culture 'which makes it OK for people to ask for help.'

PS: I give my team space to grow and develop, and offer them formal training, but everyone has responsibility for their own learning, and to create their own 'brand'. I have my own personal development plan which, apart from formal training and reading, also consists of a network of people, inside and outside the organization, with whom I arrange coaching sessions, and who regularly give me frank input and tell me how it really is.

LEON SADLER

Consulting Manager, SAP

Leon Sadler is the manager of consulting in the UK for SAP – the huge international software company which provides corporate systems to many large organizations. In his mid-thirties, Leon has an enviable career track record. 'I have been doing the same job for two years, which is a first for me!' he told me.

LS: My career began with disappointing A levels. I discovered girls and fast cars at the time when I should have been working for good grades. I therefore ended up doing a course called Manufacturing Systems at Hatfield Polytechnic. It comprised work on several MRP (Manufacturing Requirements Planning) systems, with practical in-company placements. People often say they barely use 10 per cent of their degree – I have used at least 90 per cent of mine!

Anderson Consulting came to Hatfield on the milk round and Leon joined them, rising through the ranks over the next four years. He then joined a small software company, which took a good product to market too early. 'I learned more in one year with that company than in four and a half years with Anderson. I resigned, and two weeks later, the company went into receivership.' These two events were not connected, Leon assured me!

He resigned to go to SAP as a Production Planning Consultant. From that position Leon was asked to head up the logistics consulting team of five consultants. Several promotions later, Leon now has a team of 280 staff, and complete responsibility for the UK consulting operation.

In talking to Leon, a number of things become apparent which help to explain his success. He actively seeks and uses mentors in the organization. He also networks very well: building relationships is clearly a strength. He is very open about what he does not know, and an obvious consequence of this is that it frees him to seek help from mentors or experts or more experienced staff. 'Seeking mentors is not necessarily a hierarchical thing. I go where the expertise is, at any level.' He is a risk taker. 'Better to make 100 decisions and be prepared to get ten wrong, than only to make 50.' As part of his risk taking he will take things on – and then worry afterwards about how he will cope.

AH: What are the three worst sins that a consultant can commit?

LS:

1 Not knowing when to say 'I don't know' and just winging it. It is always better to say that you'll find out.

2 Failing to deliver on your promises. If you say you'll do something – do it!

3 Not managing customers' expectations. What a customer expects from you is down to you – you can control it, so why over-commit?

On customer relationships, Leon said, 'It's a cliché, but people buy from people. In a previous company I was part of a bid team who lost a big project. Two of us were able to go back and ask them why we lost, and although we met all their technical criteria, they told us that they didn't like us! Not us individually, but the whole team, who they knew well as the team had already done some work for this client. It was quite a shock, but a salutary lesson. My approach to new customers is that I endeavour to create opportunities and give them reasons to trust me. When I'm working with a client, the aim is to be smiling, positive, never moody, never lose a sense of humour, whatever the client throws at me.'

Leon is also very aware that consultants are often drawn to the profession because they enjoy change. 'Often the people at the receiving end do not enjoy change, so our presence can be a threat to them, whether real or imagined. It's as well to hold that perspective when dealing with clients.'

Leon's advice to consultants keen to progress their career is not to make this their sole intent. 'If you push your career in people's faces it is likely to be counter productive. If you are seen to be doing things only for self advancement, then that is likely to make you very unpopular. Being part of a team is key to most roles, and someone with a focus only on their next step up the ladder will not be seen or accepted as part of the team, because people will feel that your own aims will always take priority over the team's goals.'

Leon's experience of difficult clients is summed up as a culture mismatch: 'In this company, we collaborate with clients, working with them as a team in partnership. I know that sounds corny, but that's what we do. This works very well with most clients, but a few clients have a culture where they believe that external suppliers are not to be trusted. Given this mentality, it is very difficult to do a good job for this type of customer, because of the basic lack of trust. We can only do our best to be as honest and open as possible, and consistently demonstrate our trustworthiness.'

Leon values learning very highly, and sees failure as part of the learning process. He coaches skiing as a hobby, and has a role model in John Skeddon, father of British skiing: 'Top skiers push themselves to the limit in how quickly they can learn new techniques, so they may fall down as much as one run in ten. That's quite a lot of falling down. If you are not falling over at all, maybe you are not learning, not growing, not pushing yourself as hard or fast you could be. I expect to "fall down" or make mistakes fairly often – it's a good sign.'

When asked to what he attributed his success, he said that he did not really see himself as successful; he is dedicated to doing a really good job of whatever he is doing now, and does not have a long term focus on a career ladder. This response matches his learning philosophy – success is an end point, whereas Leon is on a journey like the ski slope – always pushing himself towards further growth.

DAVID MITCHELL

Head of E-Business Practice, Oracle

David has held a number of senior consulting positions in his three and a half years at Oracle, the major software company, with responsibility for teams of over 150 consultants. Currently he is responsible for the strategically most critical consulting group – the E-Business team.

'There are two types of consulting,' David told me, 'Expert (or content) consulting is where you have the know how. Process consulting is where you understand the process of consulting to enable you to help your clients come up with their own answers, without being an expert. It is vital that clients are part of this process. My current organization combines the two types, and this is a very powerful proposition for the client.'

David's career began with a degree in geography, followed by a second degree in social geography and additional study of geographic information systems (GIS). As part of this degree he studied riot control, working with the police in Brixton – not something he has applied directly in his subsequent career, he commented. After becoming a university lecturer for a while, he decided to move into industry, and joined Bartholomew's, best known for their maps, to work on GIS systems. From there he went to Unisys, and then on to Coopers and Lybrand before joining Oracle.

'It was at Coopers that I received my "real" consulting training. They had a simple model:

- Listen
- Think
- Consult (with your colleagues, not the client)
- Act (note this is only 25 per cent)

'In my book, consulting firms are called this because they consult each other, not their clients. This is the leverage that big firms have.'

If you do not follow the sequence you may fall into what David eloquently expressed as 'premature elaboration!' The obvious example of this is the young consultant, not long out of university, who feels a great pressure to deliver value for their very expensive daily fee, and rushes in with answers without even knowing the questions!

AH: What is your career advice to consultants?

DM:

◊ You need to learn consulting as a profession. It's not just being an expert. You tend not to be taught those skills in supplier consulting organizations. Do a proper apprenticeship in one of the big consulting groups – learn the process consulting skills.

◊ On the other hand, don't join one of the big consulting groups unless you've got something to contribute. If you join straight from university, you will be given fairly basic things to do because you are not proven. If you have industry expertise, it's much better. Having some experience in industry in a non-consulting role is good.

◊ If you are a technical guru, you can go straight in, but you are unlikely to go anywhere senior without full consulting skills. It's quite a fine art to decide what to do when.

◊ If you go into one of the big groups, go with your eyes open and see organizations as they are and not as you want them to be. Lots of their business is very basic work, delivering systems – it's not all board level strategic stuff. If your expectations are too high, you will get frustrated when you find yourself writing sets of user procedures for the maintenance department of an electricity company!

🖉 Work out how long you want to be there. Is it two years for the experience and a badge for the CV or five years for that plus some seniority, or is it your end profession? Be clear on what you want to get out of it, otherwise you may drift and not get what you need. Proactively manage your career.

🖉 Expect hard work and social disruption – it is not a nine to five profession. You must be clear on that before you go into it. Note that many of the best insights into a consulting project happen in the bar after work. It's easy to find yourself doing nothing but work. You need, however, to learn how not to kill yourself with overwork, and to balance your lifestyle.

Note also that the further you go up the ladder, the more the job becomes a combination of sales and delivery, which may or may not be what you enjoy doing.

🖉 Finally, a key point about being in your comfort zone. As a rule of thumb, if you are not petrified twice a week, you are not stretching yourself enough as an individual, and in what you can do for clients. If it's too easy, you are not trying hard enough!

COMMON SUCCESS FACTORS

You will hear more from Penny, Leon and David in other parts of the book, just as you will be introduced to other successful role models in other chapters. In advance of that, let us look at common factors in their success.

Learning

Common to all the consultants is a commitment to learning. As Frank Milton, a partner at Price Waterhouse Coopers, put it, 'You need fluency in business, and you need currency – what's happening now, and what are the future trends.' David Mitchell ascribed part of his success to 'being a polymath', having great breadth of knowledge across many subjects.

Personal development

Beyond learning is a burning enthusiasm for self-development, whether expressed as falling down on the ski slope, or being petrified twice a week!

Interpersonal skills

Excellent interpersonal skills are common to all, resulting in the comment from some of the consultants that they are lucky with their clients. For luck read: 'I have the ability to get on with and bring out the best in even the most difficult people.'

Professionalism

This whole book is about being a professional consultant, and it would take too long to list all the virtues displayed here. Many relevant comments are quoted in the next chapter.

Drive

A high level of drive and enthusiasm means that these consultants make the most of opportunities, and are recognized and promoted for it.

Mentors

Mentors are also important, and the key is to go and find them if they do not naturally appear. Mentors are obviously most influential if they are senior, but you can find mentors at any level, and benefit from their expertise.

Self-belief

This is very evident in all they say, and as Penny puts it 'you develop your own brand' which means you can easily sell yourself to a client or an employer. As David commented, 'Consultants are selling themselves all the time, whatever they are doing.'

Networking

Networking is something they all do, although, as Penny says: 'I do it intuitively, and it works well. If it were obvious that I was networking just for personal gain, such as career advancement, then people would see through that very quickly.'

Building a track record

This is linked to Leon's comment about not thrusting your career aims into people's faces. The message is again consistent: do a really good job now, build a track record, and that achievement will take you towards your next career step.

Risk taking

The featured consultants are all prepared to take risks, and 'put their head above the parapet'.

It is easy to derive some key beliefs that all these consultants hold about being a consultant, and link that to your list of presuppositions. It is not difficult to see that they would be comfortable with most of those listed in Chapter 1, not least:

- 📎 There is no failure, only feedback. (Ski slopes come to mind!)
- 📎 If someone else can do something, so can you.
- 📎 Everyone already has everything they need to achieve what they want.
- 📎 If you always do what you always did, you will always get what you always got. (You certainly won't be petrified twice a week!)

Progress now

As you read about all the different consultants described in this book, identify the one who most closely matches your role model:

1 Analyse what they have achieved and how they did it.

2 Identify the gap between their skills, knowledge and experience and yours, and incorporate that into your career plan.

3 Analyse their beliefs, and try them on for size. Act as if they were true, and see what that does for you.

CHAPTER 3

What Makes a Successful Consultant?

Diamonds are nothing more than chunks of coal that stuck to their jobs.

MALCOLM STEVENSON FORBES

We are what we repeatedly do. Excellence, then, is not an act, but a habit.

ARISTOTLE

- ⓠ **Putting yourself in the client's place**
- ⓠ **Client concerns when hiring**
- ⓠ **The worst sins a consultant can commit**
- ⓠ **Definitions of success**

There are many different answers to the question of what makes a successful consultant, and the important point is that you will have your own. You may have it now – a clear image or a strong feeling that signals success. You may not yet be sure, so test out your thinking here.

Sir John Harvey Jones: Consulting is all about interpersonal skills, in particular knowing how to tailor your advice to the optimum of what the organization will take on board and implement. It is the art of being super-blunt but telling the truth in as acceptable a way as one can, and humour helps a great deal in this process. There is nothing easier than giving advice, and nothing more difficult than implementing it in the real world. I think it is important to hold that perspective as a consultant, particularly if you are not yourself the deliverer.

Frank Milton of Price Waterhouse Coopers adds: To be really good you need:

- Fluency – in all aspects of business, as well as your special expertise.
- Currency – knowing what's happening now, and what the future trends are.
- Personality – the ability to connect with people.
- Punch – the ability to make a difference. Can you say and get away with what others would not say? (Like telling the client that they haven't got a cat's chance in hell of doing whatever!)

When I recruit a young consultant, I look firstly at the academic attainment, then for evidence of success and advancement early in the career with a good employer. Finally I look for something extraordinary on the CV, something in any field which is an indicator of their spark and drive – the personality and the punch.

Just as they say that beauty is in the eye of the beholder, so the worth of a consultant is measured by the client. You may believe that you have expertise beyond question, but if your client is not happy with what you have provided, then there is no success –

only a dissatisfied client, who may well relay their feelings about you to others. Sometimes a client wants the expert to confirm that what they are doing is right. You may think there is a better way, but that may not be what the client wants to hear.

PUTTING YOURSELF IN THE CLIENT'S PLACE

A critical skill of any consultant is to see things from the client's point of view. If you can work out exactly where your customer is coming from, and what they really want from you, you are already close to succeeding. Many clients do not hire you on the strength of your technical expertise alone; in some cases other factors are far more important. It may be that they want you to do a sales job on the board for them – that your authority and gravitas will impress, despite the fact that there are more qualified people available to them internally.

It may be that your fit with their culture is vital. If, say, they have a very aggressive style, then a delicate flower of a consultant with refined skills and no backbone will not be able to operate effectively in their organization. Becoming a cultural chameleon is a prime skill in a consultant.

An insecure client may be buying your expertise to cover his or her back. Some people need official reassurance and endorsement. It is very important to recognize this at the outset, because you will need to make sure that your client is never exposed; that he or she is always wrapped safely in the protective covering of your authority and expertise. To do really well, you will shine as much of the glory on them as you can — make the right remarks to the right people to enhance their image. This may win you more work in the long run because the client will see you as a safe supporter, which is just what insecure people need.

SIEBEL SYSTEMS

Sue Goble, Head of Consulting at Siebel Systems, stands out when it comes to identifying with the client.

Sue joined Siebel in 1996 as a Technical Account Manager, when there were only eight people in the Europe office. Now there are about 2,500, and she has a team of 100 consultants working for her.

Core to the company's commitment to the client is the quarterly customer satisfaction survey, on which everyone in the company is targeted to varying degrees. Sue emphasized that 'This company-wide focus on customer satisfaction means that if there is a problem, everybody cares about it.'

Siebel also have an implementation effectiveness survey and, even when the account has reached a level of maturity, there is still a six monthly satisfaction survey.

Surveys may be overkill for your business, or you may do them anyway. The key point is that you are really trying to step into your client's shoes, and find out how they feel at every stage. Having discovered the answers, it is what you do with the results that matters. Sue speaks of this whole process with overwhelming enthusiasm, and it is clear that Siebel want this feedback, and that they are motivated to act on it immediately and truly serve the customer.

CLIENT CONCERNS WHEN HIRING

Suppose you are going to hire a consultant today. Let us imagine that you run a department in a large company, and you have been asked to lead a project. This involves doing something you have never done before, but nobody knows that. You feel a little uncomfortable about this, but decide that the best thing to do is to bring in an expert in that area. What will you be looking for from that expert? Can you describe the person you are looking for?

As you think about the answers to these questions, think about your priorities in this situation. Jot down a list before you read on; this list will almost certainly be one that you will be measured by, when you are being considered by a client.

A Finance Director, who had commissioned many projects in his time, was asked to give his list. Here is what he came up with.

- **Integrity** is top of my list. If you can't trust them, they're no good to you.

- Same with **reliability**. It's no good having the world expert if you can't be sure they'll deliver.

🔊 Next it's **credibility**. No good being an expert if you can't convey it and impress the right people with the authority of your views.

🔊 After that it's **technical expertise**, but it needs to be intelligible – if not to me then to my staff. That's different from credibility – you can blind people with science so they believe you're the expert, but then if they can't understand a word. . . .

It is interesting to see that expertise does not feature in his top three needs. How did your list compare?

Next he was asked what concerns he has when hiring a consultant:

I often have to check if the organ grinder who comes to sell to me will be despatching one of his monkeys to do the work. That can be a problem with the larger firms.

I also worry about being taken in by some sort of façade. If I don't know their field of expertise, and that's often why I'm hiring them, then I worry that they might pull the wool over my eyes. That's when I make an assessment about integrity. The more glib they are, the more uncomfortable I get. It's such a surprise when someone tells me they don't know something.

> If it's not central, then that can be just the indicator I need that they are more trustworthy than most.

This is a very interesting comment. The Finance Director is asking for your expertise, but is reassured when you say that you do not know about some peripheral area. This is a tightrope to be walked, as other clients may well be worried that there is a gap in your knowledge, and in a different situation this could count against you. Remember this when you are presenting to a prospective client. If they know their stuff, you can talk technically as equals. If they do not know your area of expertise, think how you can appear to them to be reassuringly well qualified, and absolutely trustworthy. The reasons the client finds to trust you need to be implicit in what you say, not explicit.

On the other hand it may be that your client knows a great deal about the project content, in which case you must avoid the other pitfall, described here by Sir John Harvey Jones:

> I believe that consultants will be able to do their job better if they have had some real management experience. Without this, consultants are likely to take the theoretical view, and

generally things are not done according to the textbook, even in the best of companies.

Lots of consultants have a catch-all solution which they apply to everything, irrespective of what the client's real needs are. They also will often vocalize what the organization already knows – the classic of borrowing your watch to tell you the time.

Mark Brown, Visiting Professor of Innovation at Henley Management College, was equally concerned about the calibre of consultants in the market today:

I have a prejudice about business consultants. There are lots of people out there who call themselves consultants, but who have very little in the way of skills and experience. There are lots of second hand car salesmen in this field, and there is a huge variation between the deeply dodgy and the quite spectacular. If the medical profession operated this way, I think we'd be seriously worried about falling ill!

Given this kind of view, it makes the need for integrity and credibility even more essential.

If you are thinking that this does not apply to you, that you do not get involved in selling or even setting up a project, you just turn up and deliver technical input, well, think again!

You may be a small cog in a big project team, with no significant client contact, but there will be some, somewhere, even if it is only at the coffee machine. You are always representing your company, and just the wrong word thrown in as a casual remark can create waves of concern in the client. Whatever your role, you need to be very clear what it is you and your team are delivering to the client, and what part you play in that.

The principles, therefore, apply whether you are a project manager or a junior consultant in a large firm, or if you work alone. You are selling at least one thing in all your dealings with a client, and that is yourself. You represent your company, and so you are 'selling' your company all the time.

THE WORST SINS A CONSULTANT CAN COMMIT

Not listening to the client was top of the list: 'The single biggest skill that a consultant can learn is to listen . . .' to quote software consulting company Pecaso, and almost everyone else made the same point.

Joint top of the list was this one, best expressed by Frank Milton: 'Loss of integrity. Everything you say has to be visibly traced back to the benefit of the client and not the consultant.'

Frank extended this in a different direction: 'Being intellectually honest is very hard to do. Sometimes you know something for sure; sometimes you just have an instinct for something. Consultants can get seduced into saying things at the wrong weight, because they get used to being the experts, and so they say something categoric when really they are not at all sure.'

Janet Simmons at Pecaso put this same point in a different way: 'Misleading the customer by pretending knowledge you don't have. So you say no to the client because it's the safest option, when it could be that yes is true, and you are depriving them of something that they could have, if you bothered to find out.'

She also talked about the importance of involving the client, which again has been a critical point many consultants have made to me, although more in the sense of getting them to buy into the solution, and understand any bad news that may be coming from the project findings. Janet came from a different angle: 'It's a sin not to keep customers fully involved, so that they know all the good things that are going on, and feel part of the success.'

Mark Brown took this further: 'I see a big difference between content and process consultants. A company may get an excellent content report from one of the top consulting groups, and put it in a drawer. I deliver some content, but I also work on process with the client in a highly collaborative way, so that they feel they own the result. We develop the plot together, so that they feel they invented the plot. I say to them what goes wrong is down to me, what goes right is down to you. Another cardinal sin is arrogance. Someone once said that if a company is young and growing they need consultants. On the other hand, if the company is large and fixed in its ways they need "insultants", but they are quite likely to throw them out, because they won't want to hear what they have to say, by their very nature!'

DEFINITIONS OF SUCCESS

Your success with any client relies as much, if not more, on your skills in managing the client relationship, rather than on delivering technically. If we assume you have a good level of expertise, then the difference that will make the difference can be itemized as:

1   Your ability to see things from the client's perspective and truly understand what they want from you – which may not always be what they say they want.

2   Your ability to state clearly how you will deliver what they want, matching any of their implicit needs with implicit content from you.

3   Your ability to convince the client that you have the qualities of integrity and reliability that they are looking for, in ways that are more implicit than explicit.

4   Your ability to demonstrate your expertise clearly to the non-expert client, without making them feel disadvantaged, overwhelmed or patronized.

If you can do all these things and then deliver on them, you will be able to win business and win repeat business, and get referred business, which is the most effective route to success.

CHAPTER 4

What Do You Really Want?

Good, better, best; never let it rest till your good is better and your better is best.

ANON

Obstacles are those frightful things you see when you take your eyes off your goal.

HENRY FORD

🔇 **Do you have an absolutely clear idea of what you are aiming for?**

🔇 **Can you describe how you will be different when you have reached your goals?**

🔇 **Do you know what measures you will use for your success?**

THE POWER OF BELIEF

Look at any achievement and the message is the same: If you believe you can do it, and see yourself doing it, then you will do it. We started work on beliefs in Chapter 1, and we shall return to that. We shall also give you plenty of practical input to enhance your skills, however, in this chapter we want to help you to focus on 'winning the race', on that 'increased muscle power'. Whatever your goal, we want you to be absolutely clear about it, and to experience the outcome right now.

In sporting terms, your goal could be to win the Olympic gold medal for javelin throwing. That is a clearly defined outcome, with at least one measure of success – the medal. Other measures could be how you will feel when you win, or how proud your parents will be. The next stage in this process is to imagine how you will win; to run the whole event in your head, which ends with the medal. In doing this you will see, feel and hear the whole thing. You will experience every aspect of what you will do to succeed. Run through all this several times so that it becomes familiar, and then, when you do it for real, it will not be for the first time: you will have been there before, and the outcome is known, rehearsed and you are assured.

It is perhaps easier to do that for something as clear, focused and measurable as competing in an individual sporting competition. Being a consultant is far more complex; there are unpredictable people interactions that may affect your performance, which mean many permutations of the route to success.

CREATING A COMPELLING GOAL

Defining your outcome is so important. What exactly does consulting excellence mean to you? In the case of Kay, who we met in Chapter 1, it is all about giving presentations. She feels comfortable in the consultant's role, except in this one area. For her, imagining the result is the challenge. She would like to see herself 'doing a Nigel': being relaxed, fluent and witty, holding the audience in the palm of her hand. She feels this is too big a stretch for her in one go. She will save that for stage two. Her stage one vision is a confident and fluent presenter, well received by her audience.

Progress now

Take some time to work out what it is that you really want to achieve. If you feel uncomfortable about doing this, that is an excellent sign that you really do need to do it! If you have a long list, then prioritize, and take the top two for now. You can come back and deal with the others as you progress.

When you have an absolutely clear view of your outcome, try 'going there' and imagining what it is like.

Step into your outcome

'Stepping into' your successful outcome is an excellent test of how clear you are, and it will give you more information than you expect. You may want to make some notes so that you can see the outcome more vividly when you return to it. Create a really clear picture in your mind, then step inside it and see what happens. If you have difficulty creating mental pictures, perhaps an impression with feelings and sounds would work for you. You need to be sure of the outcome and be able to move into that world to experience the feelings, hear the sounds, see what is around you and know that this is where you want to be, and that this is where you can be.

Kay does not expect applause after a client presentation, but she does 'hear' those positive murmurings that you get when someone has just impressed you. She also 'sees' approbation in the eyes of her colleagues. She 'hears' the interest in the clients' voices as they ask her questions. She 'feels' confident as she gives quick and easy answers. She 'sees' the nods as her replies are accepted. She sits down with a wonderful feeling of accomplishment, reinforced by the sense of approval she gets from the people in the room, both her clients and her colleagues. She delights for a few moments in her glory, and freezes her image right there.

Measures of success

This is a very clear outcome and it contains measures of success. Kay can now describe how she will feel when she succeeds and how her audience will react. She might want to add other measures. She might ask a colleague to give her feedback after the meeting; she might want a compliment from one of her colleagues whose opinion she values, provided that she knows they are capable of giving compliments. Some people never do, no matter how well deserved the compliment would be; if she sets that as a measure with someone like that, she will never reach it!

Getting the measures clear is a key part of the process. If you set measures which are outside your control, such as the one above, you may be setting goals which are unrealistic, and a permanent barrier to success.

A positive frame

You may have noticed that all of the outcomes Kay imagines are framed positively. Kay, who wants to be confident in presentation, is not aiming to reduce her nervousness; she is aiming to be confident. This may seem obvious, but you may often tend to express what you want in negative, rather than in positive terms:

'I want to escape from this awful weather!' rather than, 'I'd love a holiday in the sun.'

When you define your outcome(s), be sure you are moving towards the sun, not running away from bad weather. The reason for this is simple. Aiming for the positive gives you a much clearer focus, and takes you to success faster. Imagine this conversation:

'I just want to be a better consultant.'

'What does that mean?'

'Well, I'm not as technically capable as I should be, so I want to be better qualified, and I somehow don't feel my image is right, so I'd like to change that somehow.'

'So what do you want?'

'Better qualifications and a better image, I suppose.'

'How could you express that positively?'

'I want to get the chartered qualification and look like a serious professional!'

Before you read on, make sure that you have created one positive outcome, with measures for its success. If you have not done this yet, do it now!

Testing Kay's outcome

You now have the opportunity to apply some tests to Kay's outcome, to ensure that it is solid and achievable. You can follow Kay's presentation skills as an example throughout. Use the questions to fully define your own outcome.

Would you like it in other contexts?

Kay certainly would! She has been invited to speak at conferences before, and has always turned down the opportunity. Furthermore, there are social occasions where she would like to have this skill available to her.

What is important to you about achieving this outcome?

Kay is ambitious and she knows that this will be an important career hurdle for her to overcome to make her way up the ladder.

What is the real problem?

Kay is nervous and self-conscious when speaking to a group.

Is the outcome within your personal control?

Yes.

How is your present state useful to you?

Being nervous means that she minimizes the amount of exposure she gets, so she reduces the potential to make a fool of herself as much as possible. Every change you make means losing something that is useful to you right now.

Is the reward for the achievement of the outcome enough to compensate you for the loss of how things are now?

Kay is scared, but she is forced into giving more client presentations; the only option is to sacrifice her career in order to avoid any kind of public speaking. She is too ambitious to give this up, so the reward for achievement will be worth it.

Is the outcome representative of who you are and who you want to be?

This outcome is exactly in line with Kay's career aspirations. She is very comfortable with this question.

Is it worth what it takes to get it?

Kay has no doubts. You may need to check your own answer carefully.

What resources do you need, both physically and mentally?

External sources of information and guidance and time and courage.

What action steps can you commit to? Especially the first step?

Kay is going to finish reading this book, and she is going to talk to Nigel about voice and confidence training. Think carefully about the first step.

And what will help you to maintain it?

Kay would like to find a mentor, someone she can make a fool of herself in front of, and not worry about it.

TESTING YOUR OUTCOME

Now work through these questions yourself, to test your own outcome.

What is your outcome?
Would you like this outcome in other contexts?
What is important to you about achieving this outcome?
What is the real problem?
Is the outcome within your personal control?
How is your present state useful to you?
Is the reward for the achievement of the outcome enough to compensate you for the loss of how things are now?
Is the outcome representative of who you are and who you want to be?
Is it worth what it takes to get it?
What resources do you need, both physically and mentally?
What action steps can you commit to? Especially the first step?
And what will help you to maintain it?

If you are happy with the answers to all these questions, then you have a 'well-formed outcome', which will deliver success. If you find difficulty, particularly in balancing the rewards of change against staying as you are, then work on those issues. If you ignore them and just carry on, the chances of success are clearly lower.

Find an outcome that delivers greater rewards than those you get from staying as you are. It may be that you do not change the outcome at all; you may focus on those rewards, enhance them, find more of them or see more disadvantages in not changing. However you do it, the end result will clear your path to success, and remove any nagging doubts from the back of your mind. Then you can go for it!

CHAPTER 5

Valuing What You Have Now

Where talent is a dwarf, self-esteem is a giant.

J. PETIT-SENN, *Conceits and Caprices*

Use what talents you possess: the woods would be very silent if no birds sang there except those that sang best.

HENRY VAN DYKE

- Do you value what you already have?
- Do you treasure your resources?
- Do you know what you are good at and know how to increase your choices?

ASSESSING YOUR RESOURCES

Ken works in the marketing department of a finance company. He knows everybody and if you ever need a contact, you go and ask Ken. He thinks nothing of it – in his eyes, he just 'keeps in touch with a few people'.

Like Ken, we can often undervalue skills that, for us, require no effort. We think nothing of being able to run up a spreadsheet, or dash off a report. It is vital to get an objective view of these skills.

It is also important to obtain feedback on a skill that you may think that you are good at, but, in reality, you may not be. This may be harder because you may be completely unaware of your shortcomings. Start with someone you can trust to give you some honest answers to some straight questions.

Irene Nathan is clear that you need feedback at any point on the learning curve: 'I view my professional career as a continuing learning process. It is easy to get stuck in your own time warp, and think that you have the perfect solution worked out. It is important to acknowledge your own change too, and the impact that has on the work you do.'

Progress now

It may be helpful to list the skills that you have identified as essential to your role as a consultant. Here is a suggested list which can highlight your area of competence, and those skills that you need to work on.

- Specialist expertise
- Project management
- Client management
- Working as part of a project team
- Managing personal development
- Projecting the right image
- Building client relationships
- Influencing skills
- Negotiation skills
- Managing conflict
- Political awareness
- Running client workshops/project meetings
- Presentation skills
- Report writing

OBTAINING FEEDBACK

Now show the list to your boss, a few colleagues and several clients for their honest comments.

The right people to ask are those who see you operating in your consultant role, whose judgement you trust, and who are capable of being honest with you. Ideally, at least one of these people should be a client, perhaps a long-standing client with whom you feel comfortable enough to have a conversation like this:

'I'm working on a personal development programme at the moment, and I'd appreciate some input from you. Are there any areas of my role where you think I could improve? Things that I could have done better for you?'

This may lead into a conversation about your specialist expertise, which is fine. If it stops there, continue as follows:

'Thanks for that. Now is there anything on the non-technical side that you can think of?'

If this does not produce anything, prompt with:

'What about the personal side, wheels I might have oiled, people I might have managed better, that sort of thing?'

If nothing is forthcoming after this, then you will probably want to stop, unless you know them really well and can cajole them further. Many people are very reluctant to give negative feedback and get very upset if forced into it.

This applies to colleagues and, sadly, to managers too, so bear this in mind when asking them to be completely honest with you. Make it easy for them to say negative things nicely. Asking them how you could improve is far better than asking them to tell you where you are failing. Offer them prompts on a plate:

'I have this feeling that I could sharpen up my presentation skills. Do you think that would be a good idea?'

Do not say 'I feel I'm useless at presenting – what do you think?'

You may find that you need to ask different people about different aspects of your role. This puts less pressure on them as they are only required to comment on one area. You may arrange with them in advance to give you specific feedback. For example, if they are running a client meeting with you, tell them beforehand that you would like detailed feedback from them afterwards.

RECEIVING FEEDBACK

Just as giving feedback is a skill, so is receiving it. The best way to view feedback is as pure data, neither good nor bad, which you can choose to accept or reject at your leisure. Avoid at all costs the acceptance or rejection of the giver. Almost as bad is to accept or reject the feedback as it is given. Most people find giving feedback hard and giving negative feedback very hard, so bear that in mind when you are suffering at the receiving end.

All you need to do is receive it, make sure you understand it, and then take it away to examine later. Do not offer denials, excuses, defences or emotional response to the giver. Thank them for doing you a favour that you know they find difficult. Ask if they will give you more feedback later, when you have had a chance to work on improving whatever it is. It is vital that they feel that you appreciate and value their input, in order to encourage them to give you more. This is a time when you think of them, you can focus on *you* later when, alone with a box of tissues or a bottle of wine, you think about what they have said and feel the pain!

When you have felt the pain you can then move on and decide what you are going to do with this information, because, as you know, there is no failure, only feedback, and it is there to help you learn and improve.

Positive feedback

Although giving positive feedback is easier than giving negative, many people struggle to do it, so it is important to express your appreciation. It is also important to receive it gracefully. If someone tells you that you are a brilliant presenter, do not brush it aside, instead say a straight 'Thank you!' with an expression of pleasure, if not enthusiasm.

Progress now

Make a resolution to look for an opportunity to give someone positive feedback every day of your life. Also resolve that if you do not find something that merits a positive comment, you will not give it — you will only ever be sincere. This positive feedback need not be a life-changing piece of information. It is often in the small things of life that you can give a great deal, and receive even more in return.

Value what you have

When you have gathered all the feedback you can, take stock of your strengths and celebrate them. Do not dismiss them as 'the bits you do not need to work on.' Allow yourself to enjoy your prowess for a while and to gain confidence from it. This is the final stage of fixing and reinforcing the foundations before you start to build. It is vital that your base feels entirely secure.

Now you are ready to build. If you feel in any way daunted by the task ahead of you, for example, if you are preparing to run your first client meeting or give a major presentation and you get those scary feelings that are often associated with taking a major personal step, then think back to your firm foundations. If you have come this far, then you can go further – you are completely committed to a clear outcome, so away you go!

Progress now

1 Seek feedback, both positive and negative, about yourself as a consultant.

2 Pay special attention to the process of getting this feedback – it is precious and people find it difficult to give.

3 Give positive feedback whenever you can – it will generate feedback in return.

4 Celebrate your strengths, and recognize them as your secure base.

5 Identify the areas you will work on to build from your secure foundations.

CHAPTER 6
Strategies for Making it Happen

They can conquer who believe they can.

VIRGIL (70–19 BC)

The real voyage of discovery consists not in seeking new landscapes, but in having new eyes.

MARCEL PROUST

- ⦿ **Act as if**
- ⦿ **Positive energy**
- ⦿ **Check your language**
- ⦿ **Sight, sound or feelings**
- ⦿ **Learning styles**
- ⦿ **Role models**
- ⦿ **Mentors**

You now have your outcome, and this chapter offers some tools and techniques you can use to get there. You already have one tool kit – your set of presuppositions, particularly those around your personal resourcefulness.

- ⦿ There is no failure, only feedback.
- ⦿ If someone else can do something, so can you.
- ⦿ Everyone already has everything they need to achieve what they want.

ACT AS IF

A particularly useful extension of these presuppositions is not only to hold them for a while, but also to act as if they are true. If you do this, two things will happen. First, because you know you are only acting 'as if', it is easier to do than trying it for real. Secondly, the brain responds to physical signals and if you really smile, as opposed to a plastic grin, this sends a positive signal to the brain, which will then create a feeling in your head that corresponds to that smile, even though it knows you are only acting 'as if'.

When Kay stands up to give her presentation, she is acting as if she is as proficient and relaxed a presenter as Nigel would be. She is not trying to be Nigel; she is just taking on the easy confident way that he has, and she finds that as she is acting relaxed, she actually feels easier in herself and can relate more easily to the audience. Afterwards a friend compliments her:

'That really went very well, Kay. You seemed relaxed, and that made for easy listening.'

You know who you are and what you think and feel, but it is easy to forget how little of that you share with others. We imagine it seeps out through osmosis, but although some of it may, it is your behaviour that people see; if Kay gives a relaxed and confident presentation, she is a confident presenter in their eyes. This means that acting 'as if' can have immediate and very real results.

So far as the other people are concerned, you are your behaviour; so far as you are concerned, you are your thoughts and feelings.

PETER HONEY

POSITIVE ENERGY

Another technique to enhance your resourcefulness is positive energy. Start by thinking of a time when you were highly successful. 'Step into' that experience and feel what you felt at the time. When you are really there and enjoying the success, create a little gesture to remind you of how it felt – like touching your two middle fingers – anything that you do not do normally. Practise it a few times, so that it becomes familiar. When you face a new challenge, repeat that gesture to bring back those feelings of success, so that you can take them with you into the new experience.

You probably already use the technique regularly, but only in the negative. Imagine the sound of a dentist's drill – does that trigger an immediate response? Or think of a time when you were turned down for a job you really wanted – perhaps remember reading the rejection letter. Do those feelings come flooding back? Not surprisingly, you can do just the same with positive feelings as you can with negative ones.

CHECK YOUR LANGUAGE

It is really helpful to check your use of four-letter words, like 'can't' and 'must'.

Equally damaging are 'should' and 'ought'. If you find yourself using these words in expressions like 'I should do something about that report' or 'I ought to rehearse my presentation' it means that your commitment is in question. Who is telling you to do these things? It sounds like you are hearing the voice of an annoyed parent, telling you to do your homework!

If you are truly committed to something, then you will say, 'I want to do this', 'I'm going to do . . .', 'I shall be . . .' If you find yourself slipping into musts and shoulds, ask yourself the question 'Is this what I really want?' If it is, and you still feel a 'should' coming on, revisit Chapter 4. Getting this bit right is fundamental to your successful outcome.

SIGHT, SOUND OR FEELINGS?

The next tool relates to the way you assimilate data, which will be significant in your learning of any new subject. The majority of people prefer to gather information **visually**, hence the saying 'a picture is worth a thousand words'. If you can easily form pictures in your head, use that facility when you learn something new. Use pictures wherever you can to reinforce your learning.

Other people may assimilate information primarily through what they **hear**. They may or may not form clear mental pictures, but sound is easily recalled with clarity and fine distinction. If this applies to you, a tape of a new subject might be an excellent way of reinforcing your learning. Consider making your own if the subject is important enough.

Finally there are some people for whom **feelings** are their strongest sense. This does not mean they are emotional, just that they are finely tuned to peoples' feelings, including their own. Sounds and pictures may be part of the assimilation process; pictures are often unclear, with feelings attached to what they see. If you fall into this category, a priority when learning will be to associate feelings with the subject matter. This may not appear to be an easy thing to do with business or technical subjects, but a good way for you to learn is through case studies, where problems arise and are solved, and you can associate with and remember the feelings of those involved in triumph or disaster.

LEARNING STYLE

Another tool, which you may wish to investigate, is to discover your individual learning style, as defined by Peter Honey's matrix. With a questionnaire you identify which of four categories of learning style fit you best. The two ends of the spectrum are the theorist, who likes to learn all the theory before doing anything, and the activist, who prefers to plunge in and try things without any theory at all. Knowing which suits you best can greatly enhance the learning process. Details are provided in the references section at the back of the book.

ROLE MODELS

Actively seeking role models can be a great aid to the learning process, and we have included a selection in this book. Sadly, good role models are not always in plentiful supply and sometimes you need to learn from the negative as much as the positive. Take every learning opportunity that you can – most people have something to offer, whether to emulate or to avoid!

When you find someone to learn from, try to understand their attitudes and beliefs, as much as their behaviour. For example, if you see someone delegating well, find out what they believe about delegation and how they view the people they delegate to, as well as what steps they go through when deciding what to delegate and to whom.

If you have difficulty in delegating, it might be less because you do not know how to, and more because you do not have faith in the people you would be delegating to. If you could take on the beliefs of a good delegator, and act as if they were true for a while, you might find this would produce a new result, whereas just studying the methodology might not do very much at all.

Be open about your learning in this context, in order to obtain as much information as possible. You will probably already have observed the skill for a while, so you will have some information, but do not treat your role model as if they are just a creature to be observed at a distance. Ask for a personal meeting with them and tell them exactly what you want. They are sure to be flattered, since imitation is the sincerest form of flattery, and they are likely to be very willing to help you.

When you have your meeting, at a time your role model has chosen, make the most of this opportunity. Prepare some questions in advance, and keep them open so that you obtain as much information as possible, for example:

- Can you tell me about the process you go through?
- What are your beliefs about delegation?
- How do you view the people you delegate to?
- What problems have you had with delegation in the past?
- What mistakes do you see other people make when they delegate?
- How do you know what to delegate and what not to?

Make your list as long as possible. You may not use all the questions but they are there if you need them and, more importantly, they have helped you think the process through.

If you have the luxury of more than one role model, you might be able to go through this process again, and compare.

MENTORS

The final item in your tool kit is also often under-utilized: it is the ability to know when and from whom to ask for help. Many people think that there is some great virtue in doing things unaided, but you might consider it arrogant not wanting to benefit from the experience and knowledge of others.

> Learning from experience is the most important of all the life skills.

> PETER HONEY

Consistent in the career development of almost every consultant is the mentor. Whether in the business or the personal context, they have all been important.

Mark Brown, himself a distinguished professor, author and public speaker, spoke with great enthusiasm about a famous personal mentor:

'Tony Buzan [best known as the inventor of mind maps] has been an inspiring mentor for me. He has a fantastic view of human potential. He taught me how to present, inspire and enthuse people.'

Leon Sadler of SAP UK Ltd spoke in the same way about his skiing instructor, John Skeddon. Yet mentors do not have to be famous or wise people to sit at the feet of. A friend or someone junior to you may have a particular skill, insight, or just the ability to listen, which will meet your need, after all, as Peter Honey says, 'Life is just one learning opportunity after another.'

Progress now

Now that you are committed to your outcome, use these tools to get there:

1 Act as if your presuppositions are true.

2 Use the positive energy from your past achievements to help you in the present.

3 Use your language as a commitment check.

4 Assess your most effective learning method and style.

5 Make the most of role models, positive and negative.

6 Find personal mentors and nurture their feedback.

CHAPTER 7
Client Project Management

Plans are only good intentions unless they immediately degenerate into hard work.

PETER DRUCKER

He who asks a question is a fool for five minutes; he who does not ask a question remains a fool forever.

CHINESE PROVERB

- 🕦 **The project manager**
- 🕦 **Scoping the project**
- 🕦 **Setting the specification**
- 🕦 **Creating the project framework**

We look first at the role of the project manager, and then at the critical factors in setting up a project: the scope, the specification and the framework.

THE PROJECT MANAGER

What skills are needed by a project manager?

STEVEN HUNT

The Design Manager of MWH speaks from long personal experience:

'You need to understand people and be able to delegate well. It's important not to be afraid to let go of the technical detail and, increasingly, I see projects in the widest focus. I need to develop trust in the team and I need to earn their trust so that they know that I'm there to support them. They need to trust me and know that if something should go wrong, I will help them to recover the situation without apportioning individual blame. If something fails, it is normally a systems failure, rarely the fault of one person.'

He went on to describe a particular challenge he faced.

'I was asked if I would go and work in Kuwait, shortly after the Gulf War. A number of people had already turned this job down, but I saw it as an opportunity, and off I went, at 29, as Senior Design Engineer to manage a project team of Poles, Syrians, Lebanese, Pakistanis and Indians, many of whom were in their 50s. It was a challenge to win the respect of these people, but I did it through being confident of my own technical abilities, and through dealing with everyone in a very professional manner.

'It was a cultural challenge, and the most difficult situation arose when I asked a Lebanese engineer to check some of my calculations. This man was excellent, but did not have formal degree qualifications. I was astounded when he told me he could not do it, and became very upset. The next day he came in and said that as he was not qualified, he would no longer do design work, just draughting jobs. He was immovable on this, so I went along with his wishes until I contrived a situation where I had sketched out the very basics of a design, which I gave to him and asked him to draught what he could, as I had to rush back to London for a week. I returned to find the job completed – design and drawings – and after that the relationship was restored. I had obviously infringed some cultural taboo in relation to hierarchy which I was completely unaware of, and had felt my way back to restoring the relationship. To date, I've always been fortunate with the people I've worked with, and I have experienced very few major problems on projects.'

Steven is not the only consultant to have made that remark, and this 'good luck' seems to stem from a high level of interpersonal skill, combined with a very open and honest manner and a high degree of personal integrity.

On the three worst sins of a project manager, Steven begins with blame:

- ◎ Blaming people if something goes wrong. I start by looking to see what I did wrong.

- ◎ Failing to accept responsibility is another sin. The buck stops with the project manager and you must accept that.

- ◎ Failing to plan is the last one; this can result in having to make unreasonable demands on people, which is unacceptable.

David Mitchell from Oracle UK Ltd had a slightly different angle on the subject:

There are two key types of project manager. If you consider a project to be a big rock, some are good at cracking it into boulders and then get bored at the thought of gravel. Some are great at turning boulders into gravel, but can't break the big rock to start with. They are the ones who will happily tick off every tiny task. If you take a £100 million project, it would be rare to get someone to span the lot, so we play to the strengths of the individual to meet the project need.

Another characteristic of a project manager is the ability to drive a project to meet deadlines. This is normally a strength, but Mary Hill, Services Director of Pecaso, a software consulting company, talks of some difficult project managers her organization had to deal with, and this one took drive to an extreme:

> She was the best and the worst project manager! She was determined to meet the project deadline at all costs, so she did everything to make it happen, pushed things through, made so many compromises. She met the April date very precisely, and off she went. Then because we are very committed to working with a client, not just doing hit and run projects, we spent several months afterwards working with the client to unpick everything and make it really work.

Progress now

- Be clear on the project needs for big picture versus detail, and match individual strengths accordingly.

- Drive the project forward, but not at the cost of project quality.

- Take full responsibility – the buck stops with you.

- Plan, plan and do more planning – make it your aim never to make unreasonable demands on people as a result of your failure to plan.

- Set a personal example to create team values of trust, respect, loyalty and commitment.

SCOPING THE PROJECT

This section covers the earliest stage of a project, before the specification is agreed, and looks at how you decide what you are going to deliver.

The ready-made solution

One of the most consistent messages when talking to consultants is the need to empty your head of preconceptions when you are briefed by a client.

This is beautifully illustrated by Peter Honey of Peter Honey Learning, who tells a story about a very early experience in consulting with a manufacturing company in the north of England. They produced sensitive equipment, which required skilled assembly work in calibrating a fine metal bar. They had discovered over time that few people could perform this task well.

The owner of the company was very keen to devise an aptitude test for this task. This was Peter's brief, which he accepted with alacrity, being already sure that a simple hand to eye coordination test would do the trick.

He duly administered this test and it did not produce a result. Bemused by this, he decided that the differentiator could be intelligence, so he administered the tests and discovered that it was not. Now seriously worried, he decided that personality must be the factor he was looking for. He discovered that it was not.

By now Peter was very concerned. He had run out of options and discovered nothing at all. He was contemplating admitting defeat and went to the pub with a friend for some sympathy and commiseration. His friend provided more than this and asked him if he had tried the dotting test. Peter had never heard of it. It consisted of giving the individual a page of small marked squares, and asking them to put three dots in as many squares as possible in sixty seconds.

Peter tried this and, to his great relief and surprise, it worked. He took his solution to the Managing Director who was delighted. He now had a really simple aptitude test, which would make huge savings in training time.

Key messages

Peter was left with a number of conclusions, the first being that he should not have assumed that he had the hand to eye coordination answer ready-made in his portfolio of solutions. It was mainly luck that saved him from failure in this instance, although you could argue he influenced his luck by choosing the right drinking partner!

His other conclusion is very interesting. To this day, he does not know why the dotting test works – only that it does work very well. It is easy to be mesmerised by the 'why', but in many business situations, it is the 'what' and the 'how' that matter to the client.

The presenting versus the real problem

However, the 'why' does matter at the investigation stage. Another of Peter's fundamental tenets is never to accept the presented problem without investigation. This is demonstrated very well by a client's requirement for a training course. It is often the case that running a training course is seen as a solution to other, more fundamental problems.

Peter's client had asked him to design and run a course for the senior management team on chairing meetings. Although Peter asked what was behind the need, nothing further was forth-coming. He therefore asked to sit in on three meetings chaired by different managers, in order to help him to specify the need. The client agreed and Peter duly attended the first meeting, which went relatively well.

The second meeting, however, was a complete disaster and the manager concerned made every mistake in the book. He was an overbearing individual and no one dared to tell him anything he might not want to hear. He would regularly get angry and shout at his team and a few moments before he did this he would tap his pencil sharply on the desk. Peter observed this consistently over the morning and, when the meeting broke for lunch, Peter ate with some of the team. They moaned about their boss, saying how unpredictable he was. Peter said, 'He's very predictable in one thing – he always taps the desk with his pencil before he loses his temper.' No one had noticed this and all were keen to observe it for themselves.

Not surprisingly, when it happened again in the afternoon, there was a reaction from the team which the manager noticed. At the end of the meeting he asked for a private word with Peter (who was expecting to see the pencil come into action), and simply asked for feedback, as well as an explanation of the team reaction. Peter explained about the pencil and gave him some very straight feedback.

Peter expected to be thrown out, but the manager received the feedback well and was, Peter realized, grateful to get it. He commented, 'Everyone is starved of feedback, people do not get enough of it and if you have an aggressive manner, you are likely to get even less.'

Key messages

Obviously the presented problem – the need for a training course – was not the real problem, as is often the case. It is crucially important to examine the client's stated need and to check that their diagnosis of their own problem is the right one.

A second, just as vital message is client confidentiality, and thanks go to Peter for his openness in giving this example, which was a very early career experience.

Peter says:

> I committed a cardinal sin in discussing the manager with his staff. In theory it was only an observation about the pencil, I said nothing else, but it was still a breach of confidentiality, which became apparent in the meeting in the afternoon, when some of the staff reacted to the pencil tapping. As it happened, the situation turned out well, and the manager was happy to get the feedback, but it was an object lesson to me and I have been absolutely rigorous in my client confidentiality rules ever since.

Needs versus wants

A different problem arises when what the client asks for is not, in fact, what they need. David Mitchell of Oracle UK Ltd told the story of a European utilities company who commissioned Unisys to manage one of their networks:

> It had gone wrong, and the client called in Coopers & Lybrand, ostensibly to do an audit, but in reality to find reasons to sue Unisys. I worked for Unisys and I was called in to work with Coopers & Lybrand and protect our position during the audit. The findings were that Unisys had delivered what the client asked for, even though it was not what they needed. The project continued and they paid us.

What happened was that the client had given the local Unisys office a detailed specification and they had stuck to the letter, because the people there had a purely technical background — they were content consultants, not process consultants. When the client said, 'But what you've given us does not enable us to manage our network!' they replied, 'But it's exactly what you asked for'!

This highlights the dilemma for a consultant – do you give the client what they want, or what they need? Obviously as far as possible, you go for the need, which may take some courage on your part. Sometimes, that may be too big a stretch, as in the example from Mary Ahmad, of Corporate HR Partners:

Clients with a hidden agenda or a fixed idea of the root of the problem are a big challenge. I did an audit for a client and showed him the result. He told me I hadn't got it right, so I went away and rewrote it differently. This still didn't satisfy him because he had worked out the answer before he started and was going to reject anything else.

Progress now

- Listen carefully to all the client's needs and then tailor your solution to fit.
- Check that the client has diagnosed the real problem.
- Satisfy client need, rather than want, whenever you can.
- Identify any hidden agenda and tailor your work accordingly.

SETTING THE SPECIFICATION

This section covers how to nail down the specification tightly. To quote Penny Stocks of Cap Gemini Ernst & Young UK again:

> Agree with a client exactly what they are expecting. Both the deliverable and the way you will work with them. It is in this area that most litigation takes place, so it cannot be agreed at too granular a level – almost down to storyboards of the project.

The reason these problems happen is that setting objectives is about clearly seeing into the future and almost seems to be an unnatural human characteristic. We generally do not do it and yet we are very unhappy when we suffer the consequences.

You may not feel this way, in which case, you will not have a problem in pinning down goals very tightly. If you do have difficulty with this process, then think consequences. Think what happens when the client says, 'Where is it?' and you have not even started!

Objective measures

The secret is in thinking things through to the end result. The key question to ask is 'How will we know if we've succeeded?' The 'we' means you and the client separately. If the only way you know something is when the client tells you, then you are in trouble. Find objective measures at all costs. Objective measures are tools that you and the client have equal and open access to, such as calendars, production statistics and expenditure reports. The latter will not qualify if the client controls them and you cannot verify them independently.

The classic mnemonic for objectives is that they should be SMART:

- **S**pecific
- **M**easurable
- **A**chievement focused
- **R**ealistic
- **T**ime bounded

Everybody knows the theory – applying it is a different matter. Start with a date and remember that is only the start. It is too easy to think that if something is dated, it must be an objective.

Now find an objective measure, such as cost or quantity. If it is quality, beware: that usually means someone has to decide on the quality level.

It is easy to see with hindsight and the best way is to imagine the conversation you might be having with the client down the line, and anticipate any problems that may arise.

- What is the objective?
- When does it need to be completed by?
- What will it 'look' like when it is finished?
- How will we know if we have succeeded?
- What can go wrong with the end result?
- How will the client – and you – be feeling?

Let us test out an objective here.

- **What is the objective?** Online tutorial to be completed by 1 March. Untrained users to be able to access the system and retrieve personal data by using the online tutorial only.

🔄 **When does it need to be completed by?** 1 March.

🔄 **What will it 'look' like when it is finished?** Users able to retrieve some personal data without help other than from the tutorial.

🔄 **How will we know if we have succeeded?** They can access the data without difficulty.

🔄 **What can go wrong with the end result?**

> They need help to gain access.
> They cannot access the data they require.
> They require access to different data.
> They want more than just access.

Go into the future

As you think through an objective, it is helpful to take your client with you:

> So can we just imagine for a moment that we have achieved this objective, and you can see your staff, happily accessing the system, having learned from the online tutorial. They can now see their bank details. Are you happy with that?

The chances are that the client will then tell you that they do not just want bank details, and that access on its own will not be enough, they need to be able to modify them too.

🖎 **Review objective again**. Online tutorial to be completed by 1 March. Untrained users to be able to access the system, retrieve and modify the following personal data using the online tutorial only: address, next of kin, marital status, bank details.

This objective is now tightly specified.

Progress now

🖎 Take time to create a tight specification – it will pay off.

🖎 Make your objectives SMART.

🖎 Find objective measures whenever you can.

🖎 Apply the test questions to every objective.

🖎 Project yourself and your client into the future, to test out your measurable results.

CREATING THE PROJECT FRAMEWORK

Maintaining a continuing informal communication with the client is normally the basis of any project, but a formal structure is absolutely essential. The project framework specifies the formal communication processes for the project. As a minimum, these will be:

- Project milestones
- Key delivery dates
- A set programme of review meetings based around the above
- A timetable for formal written reports
- An escalation procedure to deal with problems
- A change management procedure, to cover all changes, whether chargeable or not

Critical decision-making points for this framework are the client's first requirement. They may prefer to be briefed frequently in detail or less often with a high level view. Sometimes, a client may request less briefing than you feel is right for the project, in which case you may need to suggest more meetings or reports in order to meet your responsibilities to the client.

The other factor to consider is where the project milestones fall and the timing of key deliverables. Taking the above factors into account, you can determine a sensible timescale for meetings and reports, which does not overload you, and keeps them well informed, according to your standards as well as theirs.

Imagine that this complete project framework is in place. You have a project with measurable outcomes, set milestones and a formal communication process. This is the basis of your relationship with the customer. Your relationship can be far more than this, but it should never be less.

Even if you are doing a tiny part of a huge project, you still need to know the project framework at the highest level in order to fully understand your part within it. It forms the basis of the customer's expectations and project management is all about setting and meeting those expectations. Any resetting of expectations should also be part of the formal process.

SUMMARY

1 Listen to the client – really listen!

2 Be sure you are addressing the real issue.

3 Create a tight specification.

4 Project yourself and your client into the future to test out the measurability of the objectives set.

5 Create a project framework designed to ensure the right level of communication with the client.

6 Recognize that the project manager must take ultimate responsibility for the project.

CHAPTER 8
Managing Client Expectations

Underpromise; overdeliver.

TOM PETERS in *The Chicago Tribune*

The only real mistake is the one from which we learn nothing.

JOHN POWELL

- ❧ **Over-commitment**
- ❧ **Project delays**
- ❧ **Meeting deadlines**
- ❧ **Client delays**
- ❧ **Agreeing completion**

Once the project has begun, there are many reasons why it may go off track. This chapter deals with the most common problems, and how to manage them through to a successful conclusion.

OVER-COMMITMENT

Leon Sadler of SAP makes a telling comment on this subject:

'Not managing your client's expectations is a cardinal sin if you are a consultant. You are the person who sets the expectations, not the client, so if you don't meet them, it's entirely your fault — no one else's.'

We are at the core of the consultant's world here. Expertise is all very well, but if you cannot set and manage expectations effectively, your career as a consultant is likely to be fraught with difficulty.

Noel is a young and inexperienced consultant, keen to impress. A short project is going well and he is even a little ahead of schedule, although the client is not aware of this when she asks Noel to fit in just a small piece of additional work. Noel knows that this work is not in the original specification, but it seems a very small thing – a couple of hours at the most. So, with time in hand, he readily agrees. It is not worth bothering with the change control procedure for this.

Sadly, Noel rapidly discovers that this is not a small thing. He struggles with it for three days, by which time he is behind schedule. He finally tells his manager, who gives him the predictable response:

'Noel, you should never have agreed to this – it's not a trivial task.'

'I know that now, Sara, but at the time it looked like a couple of hours work.'

'Never agree to anything outside of the specification without talking to me first. You don't have to say no to a client, just tell them you'll check and come back to them. That's not a difficult thing to say, now is it?'

Why over-commit?

Why does this go so wrong, so often, even when people are not under pressure from the client?

If this is a problem you suffer from, think about what drives you to say yes, rather than no or maybe. There are a number of likely drivers:

1   Optimism
2   Inexperience
3   Lack of planning
4   Need to please
5   Need to prove competence

1   **Optimism** is an innate characteristic which is usually a blessing! In the context of project management it is a positive curse. Discipline yourself to come up with your natural optimistic estimate, then label it as such and add a factor – like two or three times, or add in lots of contingency. Create a formula and make it a habit!

2   If you do not have the **experience** and simply do not know, then ask! Memorize the saying: 'I think that might be possible, but I'll need to check. Let me get back to you.'

3   **Lack of planning** is the easiest sin to commit of the five. Instead of listing all the details of the requirement and working through them to arrive at a time plan, take the main items, do an estimate and add on a little. Perhaps you feel that the bit you add on is quite generous and will cover it all, but in fact you may find that when you make a detailed plan, you have used up your entire contingency and more. The rule is to think through every element of the task, time each one, and add on a generous contingency. As a general rule of thumb, no task on its own takes less than half a day. This may all sound obvious in the context of producing a full project plan, but we are talking here about the additional requests, and the add-ons that people tend to ask for in a casual way, and we are therefore tempted to respond to just as casually.

4   The **need to please** will lead you down dangerous roads with clients. The way to combat this is to think of the consequences. You may please the client now by saying yes, but that may mean making them unhappy later. Better to delay saying yes, and be sure that you will keep the client happy in the long term. Again, you need the words: 'Let me just check and come back to you' on the tip of your tongue.

5   If you are out to prove how **competent** you are, you will do better to
     think long term. This was part of Noel's problem. Saying yes to the
     client made him look good at the time, but was it worth it when the
     client saw that he could not deliver? Noel had done double damage:
     saying he could do something when he could not, and failing to do
     it. He would have appeared more competent if he had said no in the
     first place.

Involving the right people

Another aspect of setting expectations is to make sure that you
set them with the right people. Penny Stocks told me of a project
where expectations had been set, but at too high a level.

Often it is the awareness of the top level relationship that
generates more resentment to you lower down the organization,
so work hard to build positive links and set expectations at all
levels.

PENNY STOCKS

Vice President, Cap Gemini Ernst & Young

A few years ago, we were working on transformation on a global scale in a very large multinational, as part of a huge project. The team had been there since January and I suddenly got a message that the HR director was seriously concerned as he felt that they had added no value for the past two months. He was proposing to put this work out to our competitors for tender.

This happened in May. I went to see him and had one of the most difficult client meetings of my career. It was a case of allowing him to give full vent to all his anger and complaints, some of which were very valid. The team had one or two weak links and had not had the best leadership. There were good reasons for this (around health and problems at home), but not ones that I wanted to present as excuses to the client. Also we had made the fundamental mistake of setting expectations with his boss, but not with him. He had been missed out of the loop.

We then had an open and honest discussion and it came down to a personal commitment between him and me. He then gave us four weeks to turn it round. This is where the support of a big firm around you makes all the difference. I was able to go back to the office and demand 100 per cent from our top people to turn this project round, and we did! We worked really hard; went more than the extra mile; we were open and honest with the client and delivered above expectations. In this process the client did recognize and acknowledge that he was also part of the problem, and waiting for two months to say anything at all was not in the spirit of good supplier management. This experience had been demoralizing for the team, but this result restored their self-respect and engaged great team spirit.

Progress now

- Never over-commit!
- Take time to respond to any customer request.
- Say, 'I'll get back to you' when in doubt.
- Under-promise and over-deliver!
- Build good relationships and set expectations at every level in the organization.

PROJECT DELAYS

Having carefully produced and agreed the project plan with the client, what do you do when, despite all your best efforts, the project goes off track and it is entirely your fault?

If you are part of a larger organization, this is where you ask for help and, probably, for more resources. If you are on your own, maybe you call in an associate or start weekend working. The critical point is what to tell the client. Assuming that you have no formal progress review meetings set up in the near future, do you advise them of the delay or hope that you can make it up and say nothing?

From the client's perspective, if you say nothing you are denying them the opportunity to take corrective action, assuming that they need to. If they do not need to know, they would still prefer to be informed, although, of course, you will lose face if you tell them. There is a very fine line between keeping the client informed and preserving your image of competence in these situations. You are making a continuous judgement about whether you will get back on track, in which case there is no need to tell, or whether you definitely will not, in which case you will want to tell the client sooner rather than later.

Progress now

- Tell the client if you know the problem is irretrievable and tell them as soon as you are sure of it.

- Tell your manager about delays early on – you will get into far less trouble that way and may get help!

- Maintain good relations with colleagues, management and client – balance your loyalties carefully.

MEETING DEADLINES

If a project plan is working well, deadlines will not be an issue. They become a problem when expectations are not reset and agreed. If you know that you cannot meet a deadline, tell your client immediately and take a revised plan to show the corrective action. This gives the client the opportunity to participate in the re-planning process. They may have an alternative that you could never have anticipated.

If the client is not meeting deadlines, you have a different set of problems to address but immediate action is still needed.

HANDLING CLIENT DELAYS

Sometimes clients drag their feet. It may be because of a lack of resources, which is more straightforward to address, but it may be lack of commitment – they know what they need, but they are reluctant to get there. Sir John Harvey Jones sums this up:

The art of consulting is to tailor advice to the optimum of what the outfit will take on board. I would always tell it as close to the bone as I thought they would accept. When I was filming *Trouble Shooter*, I was invited in because people believed they had a problem, and the fact that it was a TV programme acted as a blackmailing process on all of us, because it was in everybody's interest to achieve a satisfactory outcome.

Even in this situation, all too often one misjudged how keen they were to resolve the problem, and there was a continuing cajolery to get them to do things. Where people had an open mind and accepted the steer from me, then it was a real joy to see them taking the problem away and working on it in a way that you knew would deliver the right result.

Frank Milton of Price Waterhouse Coopers told me of similar experiences:

Clients are very reluctant to make the brave decision, and often they don't, despite all our efforts to convince them that it's absolutely right.

One client was going to implement massive organization change and install a new corporate software system. We had been working there for nine months and the time came for the client to provide the staff to work on the new software. None came. Eventually, I went to see the MD and asked him if he was serious about the project. After some straight talking, he told me that he was not committed. We stopped the project, which was the right thing to do, though painful. We were paid for the nine months' work, but the sales effort to get the deal was not recovered. I'm glad I forced the issue when I did, otherwise we could have gone through a very long and messy period which would have soured our relationship very badly. This was a clean finish, but it needed my initiative to make it happen.

Both Frank and Sir John emphasize how much interpersonal skill is needed to handle these situations. 'You need a combination of charm and grit,' Frank says, 'and humour helps a great deal, if used in the right way.'

'Humour is the shortest distance between two people', to quote Peter Honey, and is particularly relevant in situations like these.

Progress now

- Identify the real reasons why a client is holding back a project.
- Address the problem quickly and openly.
- Accept that there are limits to how far you can push a client and make a clean exit if there is no more to be done.

AGREEING COMPLETION

The project is finished; you have submitted your final report. You go to see the client for sign off, but they tell you they are not happy.

'But the project has gone really well. We've finished two days ahead of schedule. Everything is working fine. What's the problem?' you ask, amazed.

'You may think everything's working, but I'm not satisfied with the financial reports.'

Avoid a knee-jerk reaction here! This is not the time to point out that you have checked these reports against the very detailed specification. Your role now is to thoroughly understand the objections and, unless there is an obvious misunderstanding, to take them away and consider your next step. You may decide to argue, or you may make some changes just to keep them happy. You will probably want to discuss this with your manager, a colleague or a mentor.

You want a satisfied customer who views the sign off sheet with positive, not reluctant, acceptance. However, some customers make dissatisfaction a vocation or will play that game in order to squeeze more out of the project. The trick is to know who deserves a little extra effort to make the difference and who will never be satisfied, no matter how much extra you give away.

Progress now

- Know your client!
- Balance the cost of concessions against the cost of disagreement.
- Set the project criteria so tightly that scope for different interpretations is as limited as possible.

SUMMARY

1 Under-promise and over-deliver.

2 Build relationships at every project level.

3 Reset expectations early if something changes.

4 Identify lack of client commitment and act promptly.

5 Ensure that sign off will be a *fait accompli* against your tight specification!

CHAPTER 9

Avoiding Project Pitfalls

Words have a longer life than deeds.
PINDAR (522–443 BC), *Nemean Odes*

Those who stand for nothing fall for anything.
ALEXANDER HAMILTON

Having looked at the overall project process, here are some of the key elements to show what can happen when things go wrong and you end up in court!

For some very real examples of this, Gill Hunt, an independent consultant who is often called as an expert witness in court cases, was interviewed. She told me all about the legal process, which is lengthy and expensive. She also told me that during this process, most cases settle without actually going to court. This reinforces the point that resorting to law is really only good for lawyers, rarely for anyone else.

Gill says 'If you ever find yourself faced with a threat of legal action, there is a recognized alternative, set up for each business sector, in the form of a mediation process or ADR (Alternative Dispute Resolution), which is the next obvious step to take when you find that you cannot sort things out between yourselves.'

Gill gave three examples of the most typical cases. Although Gill operates in the IT field, the examples can apply to almost any commercial project.

AGREEING THE SPECIFICATION

The first is about a dispute over the specification, and she says that it is at this point in a project, more than at any other, that the seeds of a court case are sown.

GH: I was a witness for a manufacturing company who sued a software supplier because their product could not deliver on one key part of their requirement. It was a large corporate system, running across several departments. The implementation had initially gone well, but then this deficiency was discovered and, instead of raising it immediately, the supplier tried a million workarounds. Eventually they failed and the client threw them out and sued successfully.

AH: How did this get past the original specification stage?

GH: What happened was that there was a long tick list at tender stage – can your software do this, that and the other, and they ticked everything because at that general level their software could perform so they were not making dishonest claims. What did not happen was a detailed examination of what was meant by each of those generic statements, so the problem was unknown to both sides until that stage of the implementation started.

There was clearly fault on both sides here, but the supplier came off far worse in legal terms. This was a case where neither side had taken the time to clarify what exactly was needed. In fact, the client had requested a workshop from the suppliers at tender stage, but the three suppliers who were competing would not spend the two days needed unless the client paid for it, and the client would not pay. In fact, the client paid very dearly later, because what they won in court was nowhere near enough compensation for the disruption caused by having to replace the system that didn't work, and the management time soaked up by the dispute.

CONTRACT RENEGOTIATION

Gill's next example was around the need to renegotiate contract terms early in the project life cycle.

GH: This case involved a software supplier and a financial services company. The contract was to deliver a working system by July 1999 which was Year 2000 compliant. This was the requirement when the contract negotiations began in May 1998 and nothing was changed in the contract, which was finally signed six months later in December 1998!

The supplier had decided to start work in parallel with the contract negotiations to save time, but at no point suggested a change to the deadline. It was, therefore, not surprising that the code they delivered in July did not work – they had simply run out of time. The customer then put their own contingency plans into place, threw out the system and successfully sued the software supplier. You'd think it would be an obvious thing to do, to renegotiate that date, especially as it was the client who dragged out the contract signing process. I suppose they thought they might lose the business if they changed anything, but they lost it anyway, in more ways than one!

CONTRACT COVER

The last example is one where the contract did not cover all aspects of the project.

GH: There were two suppliers involved in the project, which was to provide a very specialized application in the entertainment business. The prime contractor delivered 99 per cent of the software, but a very small, very specialist piece was provided by a company with only one employee.

Initially all went well, but then a problem arose, which was found to be in the specialist software. By this time the individual concerned had left the country, taking his source code with him, and could not be traced. The prime contractor had not covered this relationship contractually, so they had no rights at all to this software and no access to the source code. This proved such a critical issue that, in the end, the client threw out the whole system and successfully sued the prime contractor.

These things seem so obvious when you're standing in court, but, at the time, people don't think. Usually there are huge time pressures – the specialist software is just a detail and is therefore overlooked. It was very unlucky that this should have had such an impact on the whole system, but that's life!

READING THE SIGNS

Gill also made the point that many companies do not spot problems early enough.

GH: Unfortunately a lot of companies don't notice until the problem is staring them in the face, by which time any or all of the following will be happening:

- ✎ Previously friendly customer staff won't talk/return calls
- ✎ The project is way over time and budget
- ✎ Staff from your competitors are visiting
- ✎ Payments for services, maintenance or other items are overdue
- ✎ The customer keeps finding new faults

The final, undeniable sign of a serious problem is the letter from a senior figure on the customer side (and we are definitely talking about 'sides' now rather than 'partnerships') or from a lawyer. By the time it has reached this stage it is going to be very difficult to resolve things without the application of money and serious amounts of effort.

PREVENTION PLAN

Gill suggested the following preventative actions:

- Don't sell what you can't deliver – try to avoid unrealistic deadlines; get a delivery specialist involved as early in the sales cycle as possible, who really understands how to estimate timings.

- Pay attention to the contract. Don't allow material to be added to the contract unless it is clear and unequivocal, for example, using the responses to an invitation to tender (ITT) when a proper specification would be better. Whatever it says in the contract is what the courts will expect you to have done. Don't rely on any understandings, gentleman's agreements or assumptions.

- All customers will do their best to get a good price. Make sure that any discount given doesn't detract from the level of service that will be provided.

- Specification – get a good, clear specification of what is to be delivered and when. If the project includes the work to produce a specification (as in a Research and Development project) make sure all changes are minuted and that there are opportunities within the plan to stop and take stock before ploughing on.

◊ Change control – make sure there is a process and that both sides use it. Don't allow the project to be pressurized into 'just doing this' to keep things sweet. Even if you decide to do a change for free, go through the process so the customer knows you are serious about keeping control.

◊ Communicate frequently and clearly with everyone involved. Make sure that people know what has to be done to make the project work. If there is a problem, say so. Make it clear what the consequences of a particular problem are, and also what will happen if a decision is not taken.

◊ Monitor the project closely and look for any signals from the customer that all is not well.

CHAPTER 10
Image

When you are content to be simply yourself and don't compare or compete, everybody will respect you.

LAO-TZU

What lies behind us and what lies before us are tiny matters compared to what lies within us.

OLIVER WENDELL HOLMES

- **What is image?**
- **Messages that image conveys**
- **View of an image consultant**

Most people make judgements about appearances. Many people make a judgement that if you have 'dressed up' to meet them, you have made an effort. This effort means that you regard them as important, and this importance means that you value and respect them.

WHAT IS IMAGE?

As well as the way you dress, image has other aspects that you can easily overlook. Hair and fingernails can ruin a good impression, both in cut and cleanliness. Cheap perfume and a harsh voice will offend other senses, and do not forget your accessories — a briefcase full of rubbish, a dirty car or a chewed pen can all count in different ways.

'I never notice details like that,' a consultant said to me, 'it's what I deliver that counts.' Many people do not notice these things, but they are very important to others. Also, although you say you do not notice if shoes are shiny or not, people often form a subconscious impression of such details. Although when we meet a prospective consultant we may not consciously register the slight stain on the tie, the dirty fingernails and the grubby shoes, we are left with an impression of a slightly scruffy individual.

This subconscious impression can then lead to other conclusions. Sue has just met this consultant, and is reporting back to her boss. 'I don't know, there was something unpolished about him. I didn't feel he was really sharp and on the ball. I wonder how focused he will be, how good his attention to detail is . . .'.

If you think this is far-fetched, then take a look at all the research that has been done on first impressions at recruitment interviews. People reach an astonishing number of conclusions about an interviewee in the first five seconds of the meeting.

THE IMAGE CONSULTANT'S VIEW

Irene Nathan is the Managing Director of the Interpersonal Relations Group and founder President of the Federation of Image Consultants. Irene founded this organization because she wanted to create a 'non-cosmetic' image for the work that she and many others do and to set standards of best practice for the image profession.

IN: If you start off in the image consulting profession, you can go one of two ways: you either stay with the looks and the superficial or you develop into a consultant for far more than the colour of a tie or a suit. Image is about who you are as a person and most consultants in the profession deal with a much bigger picture than someone's mode of dress.

AH: Do you have some advice for the new consultant?

IN: Consult an image consultant!

AH: But a new or junior consultant might not be able to afford such a luxury.

IN: Then they can volunteer to be a model on a training course for image consultants. They are often looking for people, and of course there would be no charge. The Federation website has details of recognized training providers. [See the references section at the end of the book.]

When Irene meets a new client, she spends time finding out who they are. She prompts them and then listens objectively. She will home in on their values and discover what is really important to them. When they both understand who they are building the image for, then she can begin.

IN: It is not unusual for the individual to be unclear about who they are or how they want to be perceived. For example, someone might say to me that they are looking to project more gravitas, that when they are in a new situation they feel vulnerable and this can show. Often people like this will be high achievers, but they do not place a high value on what they have accomplished. If I can help them to value themselves more, then the gravitas tends to follow and clothing is really a thin decorative veneer on the solid wood of self-esteem. It is this change in self-esteem which really delivers the image change. I can't make someone acquire self-respect, but I can be persevering and tolerant enough to help them find things in themselves of worth and value, so they are able to project in a confident manner.

If I were advising you as a new consultant, I would suggest that you find an outfit that you not only look good in, but feel good in too. These two things are quite different and the feeling good is the important point. When you are sure that you have found this feeling, slowly build a few similar items on the same theme. No need to spend a great deal of money, the important thing is that you retain this feeling, which will enhance your performance in whatever consulting role you perform.

Irene's advice on casual versus formal dress is very specific.

IN: The important thing is not to look sloppy or incomplete. People think, whether consciously or otherwise, that your sloppiness may well translate into other areas of your work. Similarly, always look current – if you appear to be out of date in your dress, they might think that also applies to your thinking.

Do not overdress or under-dress – always choose appropriate dress, and when the culture demands casual dress, go for smart casual, avoiding any suspicion of that sloppiness mentioned earlier. You are aiming, as far as possible, to look like yourself, as a business professional.

I do not play God with clients. If they tell me they will only wear designer labels, that is what I will advise them on. We can help people move from being self-obsessed to self-possessed, but knowing when to stop is a key skill in this field because it is so personal. A good consultant becomes a catalyst – someone who identifies areas that can cause a positive chain reaction.

SUMMARY

1 Avoid looking sloppy in your dress – clients may think this reflects your work.

2 Be sure that your dress is current, to match your thinking.

3 Wear clothes that you feel good in, as well as knowing that they look good.

4 Match the client's dress code as far as you can but retain the edge, and avoid straying beyond smart casual.

5 Recognize that image can convey messages (intended or otherwise) about how much respect you have for a client.

6 Be aware of *all* the physical aspects of image – your car, shoes, etc.

7 If you are unhappy about your image, consult an image consultant!

8 Image comes from within, so pay as much attention to your state of mind as to your dress. Self-belief, enthusiasm and conviction will shine through the dullest of outfits.

CHAPTER 11

Running a Client Workshop/ Project Meeting

Whether you believe you can do a thing or not, you are right.

HENRY FORD

I hear and I forget. I see and I remember. I do and I understand.

CONFUCIUS

- ◎ **Assembling the right people**
- ◎ **Briefing the essentials**
- ◎ **Facilitating a discussion**
- ◎ **Dealing with awkward questions**
- ◎ **Winning commitment**

Definition

This type of meeting is not a workshop in the training sense, it has the specific purpose of gathering data from the client, at the beginning of a project.

Objectives

Be clear about your objectives for running a workshop. When you have them written down in front of you, you can decide who the participants should be. Here is a sample set:

1   Gather specified project information from the client

2   Get everyone's views on the table

3   Give enough information to the client in order to get 1 and 2

4 Discover any issues or obstacles to implementation

5 Win commitment of participants

6 Give a positive impression of your organization

ASSEMBLING THE RIGHT PEOPLE

You will want the people in your workshop to be those best able to give you the data you need. It is worth spending time discovering who to target. Organizational structures can be misleading. Sometimes more senior people do not know enough detail, sometimes junior people do not have the big picture. Be careful that the organ grinders do not send their most junior monkey. The way to avoid this is to ensure that the client staff fully understand the benefits of investing their time. You may wish to arrange a briefing session for key staff as a preliminary to setting up the meeting.

BRIEFING THE ESSENTIALS

It is critical to share your main objectives with the people in the meeting and to give them a plan so that they can see what is required of them, and identify with the outcome. This is best presented to them in written form – on a flip chart, for example – so that they can use it as a reference point in the meeting.

You want project data from the client – that is your key purpose. To get it, you may need to give some information. This is where your presentation skills come in, but for a workshop the key point is not to get carried away. Your main aim is to gather data and you will want to give as much information as necessary to get that data and no more. You will not want the presentation to take the form of a monologue from you. Instead, break it up with questions and test people's understanding as far as you can:

'Is everyone clear on that point? I know it's a bit convoluted, so I can give another example if that would be helpful?'

Just the slightest nod from one person in response to this should tell you that you need to give further explanation. Usually, for every one person who indicates they are not clear, there are at least three others with the same problem!

You may also wish to deliver the information in small chunks, so that you cover one area at time. This is preferable, except where input does not make sense unless it is delivered in one piece. It is really important to put yourself in the client's shoes, and think what would make life easiest for them.

Another aspect you will want to consider is whether your participants have different knowledge levels. Check this carefully, and whenever possible brief everyone to the same level beforehand, or ask those who know to brief their colleagues in the meeting.

FACILITATING A DISCUSSION

It is critical that you get contributions from everyone in your meeting. Spend time discovering precisely who the participants are and, even if you find that you have people who are superfluous, it is still important to get their contribution, not for your benefit, but for theirs. If you have done the right preparation and you do not get the right people, they are still your clients and you need to win their commitment. Your aim is for everyone to leave the meeting feeling that they have contributed something useful to an outcome that they understand and are committed to. They will therefore feel motivated and impressed by you.

DAMAGE LIMITATION

Julie, an HR consultant, was called in by the MD of a company to review their compensation and benefits package. She ran a small workshop with the HR team and soon discovered that the package the company had was pretty competitive. It was not the best in the market by any means, but it did not require radical surgery. In the workshop, she discovered that the real problem was the MD himself who was highly autocratic and a very poor communicator. People operated in a climate of fear and uncertainty, which meant that the good ones did not stay for very long. The MD put this down to a poor benefits offering and told HR to fix it.

Julie then used the workshop to come up with creative solutions to fix the problem, but sadly the best solution was to replace the MD – not a practical option. They did, at least come up with a plan to counteract some of the poor communication problems, at least for the staff lower down in the organization, who could be protected from the MD to some degree. The workshop also came up with a plan of what to present to the MD, to show that the consulting project had been worthwhile. The HR team told Julie that, 'It's no good just telling him that the package doesn't need much changing. He's hired you to change it, so you need to do what he asks.' They devised a plan together.

It is clear that Julie will not be able to fix the root problem here, since the problem is the person who hired her. However, she achieved a number of key objectives by using the workshop approach:

- She gained a rapid understanding of the current situation and the real problem, with its political implications.

- She won the confidence of the HR team.

- She came up with a damage limitation plan and a proposal to give to the MD, all with the full commitment of the team.

If you can achieve the same objectives as Julie, you will be doing well, as, in your case it is unlikely (we hope) that you will be facing the impossible challenge of the MD being the root of the problem.

DEALING WITH AWKWARD QUESTIONS

Kevin's workshop started well. He has the right people there and they all seem keen. He has just finished outlining his 'route map' for the meeting, when Ann asks 'Kevin, before we start, I'd like to be clear on something that's bothering me. I understand you've never done this type of project before, is that right?'

Kevin has been with the company for six months, and this is certainly his first time. He decides to be honest.

'You are quite right Ann, this is my first time on a project of this type, although I have done quite similar work.'

'I didn't actually mean you, Kevin, although thank you for telling us. I meant your company.' She is right, and he decides to prevaricate.

'Can I just ask where you are going with your questions, Ann? I'm happy to answer them, but I'm not sure what purpose . . .'

'I just want to know who I'm dealing with. If it's a load of novices, then the information I give and the amount of checking I do will be greater than if I know you are seriously experienced in this field.'

The rest of the group nods assent and Kevin is back in the hot seat.

'Well, I think it comes down to degrees of similarity. I cannot give you a definitive answer here, but what I do know is that our company is very experienced in managing projects that are similar, and have been consistently successful. I think it is the way we work, our attention to detail and our project management skills that will deliver for you. And that is more important than whether we have done exactly the same thing for another client.'

Kevin sees a positive response from the group to his words, but Ann still looks doubtful.

'If you want a more precise answer, Ann, I can find out more detail after the meeting. Shall we talk then?'

Ann shrugs, and this is Kevin's cue to move on swiftly and hope that she does not follow this up afterwards. If she does, he will refer the problem upwards.

Kevin has succeeded in doing two key things – he has maintained integrity, by not lying about his own or his company's experience, and he has maintained credibility by placing emphasis on their working methods and track record, rather than their specific project experience.

The group are clearly happy with this response, and when Kevin sees that Ann was not, he offers her precise detail after the meeting, which makes it difficult for her to continue the debate with him. She would have appeared to be nit-picking and her shrug acknowledged that.

When faced with this type of question, it is always a balancing act between honesty and credibility. If in doubt, honesty wins, because if the client discovers you have deceived them, the relationship will be severely damaged. Better to tell the truth and lose credibility. On the other hand, there is no need to rush to the client and tell them that this is your first time when you have not been asked. It goes without saying that you would not take on a project that you were not competent to complete, so you are justified in maintaining as much credibility as you can.

WINNING COMMITMENT

Using the power of the group

Kevin was using the power of the group against Ann in this case study. They were satisfied with his response and she was not, but because she recognized she was alone, she did not press the issue further.

If someone strikes you as annoying, or nit-picking or overbearing, then the chances are that the group will think the same way. It then becomes much easier for you to say, 'Does everyone agree that we can close down the discussion on this now?', rather than trying to control the individuals yourself.

Needless to say, it also avoids personal animosity. Ann knew the group did not want to hear any more; Kevin responded to the group's need.

Reaching decisions

When you chair a meeting, one of your key responsibilities is to help the group reach a conclusion. This may also be required in a workshop. Consider the Case Study opposite.

Kevin knows it is deeply frustrating to an individual to be asked for their view, and then to have it over-ruled – particularly by someone outside the organization. A majority vote is more acceptable, but the person will still be dissatisfied. The worst thing of all is to pretend to consult and then announce that the decision has already been made, with little or no regard to the discussion that has just taken place. People see through this very quickly, and view their contribution as a charade. If the decision has been made, it is better just to announce it and not pretend you are interested in people's views, when they are clearly not being taken into account.

'So are we all agreed on Option A?'

Kevin looks round and sees general assent. 'That's fine, then, I shall record that as our conclusion. Now what about the location – I think the Brighton office is favourite?'

There are some murmurs of agreement, but Clive says 'No Kevin. John and I are firmly in favour of Bradford.' John nods agreement.

'Is there any way we can agree on location today?' Kevin perseveres.

'Sorry, but we need more information, so I think we will have to discuss it again.'

From his knowledge of previous discussions with the project board, Kevin is pretty clear that Brighton will be the final choice, but he resists the temptation to impose a decision, or to suggest a majority vote. It is critical that he wins commitment from all his clients and, for the sake of a small delay, it is not worth alienating John and Clive.

Closing the meeting

Kevin concludes his workshop like this:

> I'd like to thank everyone for their contribution. We have achieved all the objectives on the flip chart except for item 3 – location. There will be another discussion on this topic when we have more information. Now, is there anything else anyone wants to raise?
>
> No? Well then, I'll be writing to you all by the end of the week with a summary and action points. Thank you all very much for coming. I think we've made an excellent start.

The conclusion is brief: no need to go over any detail, but it is useful to summarize so that the participants feel a sense of achievement. It is vital that any deferred items are mentioned. He thanks the contributors, describes the next step and ends on a positive note, all designed to reinforce commitment and leave a positive impression of his company.

SUMMARY

When setting up and running a client workshop or project meeting:

1 Be clear on the objectives.

2 Invest time and effort to get the right participants.

3 Give them a 'route map' for the meeting.

4 Check their knowledge levels.

5 Brief them well, but only give them the information they need, and check their understanding.

6 Get contributions from everyone.

7 Use the power of the group to control the discussion.

8 Win commitment to decisions, never impose them.

9 Identify political issues, but keep any political discussion outside the meeting.

10 If you defer an item, record it and mention it at the end to reassure its owner(s) that it is not forgotten.

11 If faced with awkward questions, put integrity before credibility when you reply.

12   Before closing the meeting, check that you have met your objectives.

13   Summarize what the meeting has achieved, and define the next step.

14   Leave your participants with a sense of achievement and a positive impression of your company.

CHAPTER 12

Building Client Relationships

Listen or thy tongue will keep thee deaf.

AMERICAN INDIAN PROVERB

Everyone is kneaded out of the same dough but not baked in the same oven.

YIDDISH PROVERB

- **Listening**
- **Creating rapport**
- **Filters as styles**

This is a fundamental skill and perhaps more important if you have not been part of the sales process. In converting a prospect to a client, you are bound to have built a relationship, but when you walk into the client offices for the first time to begin the project, you are starting from cold.

Building a relationship begins with effective communication. Here is a reminder of the statistics on how we communicate:

- 7 per cent: the words themselves
- 38 per cent: how we say them – tone, volume, etc.
- 55 per cent: non-verbal signals – gestures, posture, etc.

Everyone interviewed for this book was unanimous that listening was a vital skill in a consultant, and they all had stories to tell about the consequences of not listening. From the figures above, you can see that only using your ears will not make you an effective listener.

LISTENING

Being proactive when you are listening is a skill you need to work at and involves using your whole body. If this seems a strange concept, that is a good thing, because a fresh approach to an old subject can start you on a new path.

- Your **mind** has to be completely focused on the person you are listening to, not on what you might say next or tomorrow's problems.

- Your **eyes** must collect plenty of information about the person you are talking to, from their dress to their emotional state – you should look for all those non-verbal signals. Your gaze will stay with them, and not wander around the room.

- Your **ears** are busy, not just hearing the words, but also the tone of voice.

- Your **mouth** is generally shut, but will open occasionally to offer encouraging words and sounds, such as 'Oh?' and 'Mmm'.

- Your **body** will reflect the posture of the person who is talking. If they are sitting, do not stand over them. If they are relaxed and laid back, so will you be. Do not mimic them slavishly, but match their style, so that they can see that you are in tune with them.

Progress now

This skill needs practice, so you might want to surprise your family or friends by trying it out in a social context. A good exercise is to take a social situation with someone you do not normally talk to very much. Perhaps you have little in common. Give yourself 20 minutes to find out what they feel passionate about. It might be jam making or sky diving – the point is that you do not get distracted by the subject and can focus on listening rather than talking. Consciously check what all the different parts of your body are doing. If your ears are working well but your eyes have found an interesting distraction, then bring them back to your subject and see how differently the person responds when you look at them.

CREATING RAPPORT

If someone feels that you are really listening to them, that is a great start to building rapport. There are three steps in this process, called:

1 Match

2 Pace

3 Lead

Matching means getting in tune with the person you are talking to:

🔖 Henry loves cooking. He talks of it with expansive gestures and great enthusiasm for the creative expression he finds in the kitchen. You respond with animation and frame your questions with expressive gestures.

🔖 Sally adores sky diving and, to your surprise, speaks of it in distant dreamy tones, describing a sense of peace that she finds in the silent air. You respond in tones of quiet interest, so as not to interrupt her dream. She speaks slowly and so do you.

These are examples of matching and pacing. When you are in tune with someone like this, operating at their pace, then you can start to lead them where you want to go.

In Henry's case, it might go like this:

'Just give me some chillies and a wok, and I can do anything!' (Arms thrown wide!)

'That's fantastic, Henry! I can taste those flavours now! Is Chinese your speciality?' (Hand gesture)

'I do the best stir fry ever!'

'Have you ever cooked for ten?'

In Sally's case, the pattern will be the same, although it will look and sound very different, since instead of animation and excitement, we have calm and quiet.

'It's such a peaceful experience, up there, so calming.' (Closes eyes)

'I can sense how you feel Sally – complete serenity.'

'Mmm.' Sally's eyes are still closed.

'Is it always like this?'

'Every time.'

'Even the first time?'

'Not quite the first time.' Sally's eyes open. 'There's a lot to think about the first time.'

'I thought so. How would I feel, doing it for the first time?'

Note how well Henry and Sally have been matched and paced before they are led in a new direction. The listener is there, tasting the food and feeling the serenity.

Matching can take many forms. David Mitchell told me about an experience where a colleague returned from an initial client meeting very upset indeed:

> The Finance Director was a working class Scot, who called a spade an f***** shovel, and David's colleague was a very formal Englishman — chalk and cheese just did not describe it. The client also held the belief that all consultants are money grabbing so and sos, and are therefore to be shouted at and abused to keep them in line.

> We agreed that I would take over the account, and I gave the client as good as he got — being a fellow Scot did help, but it was more the way I matched his style. In a meeting one day, the client was out of line. I took a piece of paper from my pocket and said to him,

> 'Jimmy, you know the rules of football?'

> 'Of course I bloody do!'

'Well this is a red card! You're way out of project scope, so get back into line!'

We laughed, and he did as he was told, and I had no trouble with him at all after that.

Progress now

- ✪ Practise match/pace/lead in a safe, and probably social, situation.
- ✪ Use your whole body listening skills to assess the state the person is in.
- ✪ Match that state, and pace them. For example, if they speak slowly, so will you.
- ✪ Then adjust the pace to lead them where you want to go.
- ✪ If they do not follow, go back to matching and try again.

Rapport breakers

Having examined some of the elements in building rapport, it is worth looking at some of the things that can break it. They are everyday expressions that we may use without realizing their impact. Take a look at the following interchange, and see if you can identify the problem phrases.

'Do you realize that this is a serious project issue, James?'

'I know that, Murray!'

'You should be making contingency plans. It seems to me that the whole project depends on how you manage this crisis scenario. If you take my advice, then a group crisis team could formulate some alternative outcomes, and . . .'

'Thank you, Murray, I know what I'm doing.'

'But with respect, James . . .'

'I said I know what I'm doing! Now can you just . . .'

'I hate to say this, but . . .'

At this point we can imagine that James might hit Murray!

Here is the exchange again, with the 'red rags' guaranteed to alienate and upset people highlighted.

'*Do you realize* that this is a serious project issue, James?'

'I know that, Murray!'

'You *should* be making contingency plans. It seems to me that the whole project depends on how you manage this crisis scenario. *If you take my advice*, then a group crisis team could *formulate some alternative outcomes*, and . . .'

'Thank you, Murray, I know what I'm doing.'

'But *with respect*, James . . .'

'I said I know what I'm doing! Now can you just . . .'

'*I hate to say this, but* . . .'

Assumed deficiency

🕭   Do you realize . . .

🕭   Have you thought . . .

These assume that they have not! This is insulting.

Parental language

🕭   You should . . .

🕭   You ought . . .

🕭   You must . . .

All of these are prescriptive instructions that parents often give to their children. This is not recommended between adults!

Similarly, 'If you take my advice' is thrusting the unwanted onto the unwilling.

Pompous or formal language

This is generally a real turn-off. James does not want to hear about Murray's plan to 'formulate alternative outcomes.'

Insincerity

'With respect' means the opposite!

'I hate to disagree with you' means, 'I'm going to enjoy this.'

Progress now

If you find yourself using any of these expressions, there is a solution: **respect**. If you have respect for the person you are talking to, these rapport breakers will not happen.

Imagine that this is a person who is extremely wise and talented – you look up to and admire them. If you see them in this light, respect follows automatically. You will find that there is no danger of assuming deficiencies or speaking to them like a child.

FILTERS AND STYLES

Another key element in building rapport is recognizing different filters and styles in other people. Some people are easy to get on with and seem to be on your wavelength immediately. Others feel like very hard work.

The chances are that the people you get on with have similar filters and styles to you. If you ask someone what is important to them about a business presentation, you will get some consistent remarks, such as it must be interesting and relevant, but other aspects may vary.

- 'I like a presentation to give me the big picture. If there's too much detail I get bored very quickly.'

- 'I don't agree. I like a presentation to be thorough, and you can't see the big picture unless you have all the detail there too.'

These are examples of two very different filters — the preference for detail, or lack of it, and the need to see things on the grand scale before dealing with any detail.

There are many different filters that people apply to their map or view of the world, but here are some major ones:

- Focus on detail or on the 'big picture'
- Focus on things/systems or on people/feelings
- Focus on being proactive or reactive
- Focus on looking for similarity or for difference
- Focus on the past or on the present or the future

If you imagine a client called Adam who loves detail and similarity and focuses on things rather than people, that knowledge will have a major impact on how you present a report to him. You might say:

'This is very similar to other successful implementations in parallel environments. It covers all aspects of the topic in full detail, with complete systems information included and additional references as appendices.'

This would be the opposite of what you would present to Graham who is very focused on people, dislikes detail, and looks for new ways of doing things:

'This implementation has very special features which will be unique to your organization. The report covers all the top line information you will need, so that you have a complete overview of the system. The impact on staff is highlighted throughout.'

Examples of different styles are:

🔖 **Pace** – fast or slow, relaxed or pressured

🔖 **Manner** – formal or informal

Styles tend to be easier to spot than filters but, if you are wondering how you find out about all these things, the best way is to ask. This sounds obvious, but it is something that people rarely think of doing. If the client asks for a presentation, instead of saying yes and rushing off to prepare, you could say:

'Could you run through quickly what you are expecting from this presentation?' You can also check length, and style: 'How long have we got by the way, and what medium shall we use?'

If the client has no preference, that tells you something, but if they are speaking for someone else, better to check specifically:

'Do you know how much time the MD has? Does he prefer formal presentations? How much detail?' etc.

The more information you have, the better you can tailor your delivery. If your audience is mixed, you will be addressing the politically significant client(s) and matching their requirements as your priority. If you know that there are lovers of detail in the meeting, but they are not your prime audience, tell them that they can read detail in the notes or that you can cover detail with them separately.

Progress now

Identify your own filters and styles. Ask someone who knows you well if you are unsure.

Now think about key clients or prospects and see how much you know about them. If the answer is not a lot, you might want to practise gathering data on someone reasonably 'safe' before you start in earnest. Think of someone you know, but do not get on with particularly well. Take an opportunity to meet them informally and work on your questions and observation. It is often easier to question someone about what is important to them regarding a specific work issue, rather than asking general social questions.

It is likely that you will find that you get on more easily with people who share your styles and filters, but it is an interesting exercise in itself to test this out. If they are different, you can experiment to see what effect matching them will produce – you may be surprised with the positive response that you get!

CHAPTER 13
Handling Client Politics

Man is by nature a political animal.

ARISTOTLE (384–322 BC), *Politics*

Nearly all men can stand adversity, but if you want to test a man's character, give him power.

ABRAHAM LINCOLN

POLITICAL STRUCTURE

Handling politics in your own organization can be challenging. It becomes more so when you are dealing with client politics, and often a major project will generate its own set of politics. It will involve change and change normally has its initiators and its enemies.

Most organizations have some level of politics, so the first thing to understand is the political structure. This comes in three layers, which are easiest to think of as concentric circles.

Figure 13.1 - Political structure

Inner Circle
Middle Circle
Outer Circle

This method of analysing politics was originated by Target Marketing Inc. now part of Siebel Systems Inc.

The inner circle consists of the real movers and shakers who set the culture and make all the key decisions. Note that hierarchy may not always map neatly onto these circles. The personal assistant (PA) to the managing director might be a central figure in the inner circle, as might the partner of the Chair. An excellent example of this was Nancy Reagan during her husband's presidency.

The middle circle is called the circle of influence and consists of people who understand the political structure and know that they are not in the inner circle, but have ways of influencing one or more inner circle members, and are well informed as to what is really going on. They are usually the key implementers of inner circle decisions.

The outer circle consists of people who may not know that there are circles at all, never mind which one they are in! They are the people that things happen to.

If you are in a position to draw the three circles and name the key players in the first two, you have an excellent understanding of your client, which will be a great help to you in project implementation. It would be exceptional to have all this information before you start your project, but work on gleaning whatever you can and stay alert to political issues in any situation.

If you find an opponent of the project in a meeting you are holding, find out which circle they are in, who they are allied to and the political history between their most senior ally and your project sponsor. It is also vital to know where your project sponsor sits – ideally in the inner circle. If they are in the second circle of influence, how powerfully are they connected to the inner circle? Never assume that seniority bestows power. The managing director may not be the most powerful person on the board.

POLITICAL INTELLIGENCE

The way to discover this information is to listen for clues in any client interchange. If someone says 'We can't do that, x would never agree to it,' that suggests 'x' has power', and a few follow-up questions from you can prove very fruitful. People often have much to say about those in power, usually because they are nervous of expressing their own feelings to the individual concerned, and they tell others instead.

The other way to find out about your client's political structure is to ask your tame allies within the client. Every project will have at least one dedicated supporter and they are your ally. Ask them to describe the power structure. Who are the key people to convince; who will put obstacles in the project's path? You can do this openly because it is all in the interest of the project's success.

If your prime ally is someone who does not take much notice of these things, find another ally or ask them to recommend someone to talk to. Take greater care with your questions now, unless you are sure that they are truly on your side, since you risk receiving misinformation or alienating someone who does not wish to answer this type of question. Your project needs allies and supporters; if these are thin on the ground, you need to set about winning some more! If unsure, save your political questions until you feel you are on safe ground.

Client Politics

Politics can be very difficult to handle when they are embedded in a company culture. Mary Hill at Pecaso told me of an exceptional case:

Pecaso specialize in implementing SAP HR systems, and we won this contract with a very traditional company in the North West of England. This company had a number of small subsidiaries and the implementation was complex because they had lots of small groups of staff on different terms and conditions. A previous implementation by a different supplier had failed. Two of the main board directors, although apparently very positive, played a constant political game of 'nice cop/nasty cop', with the nice cop providing the nasty cop with all the bullets.

Soon after the project began, there was a clear lack of commitment on the client side and John, the managing consultant put the project on hold, then renegotiated the terms of engagement. The situation improved for a while but, as time went on, it was clear that the client did not have the energy or the resources needed, which meant even more effort from us. When a meeting was called to discuss an issue, the priority was to allocate blame. John would say: 'I would tell them not to waste time finding fault, but just to get on with fixing the problem, but it wasn't any good, until they'd found someone to blame they couldn't go forward, it was so much part of their culture.'

The whole situation was made feasible only by the project sponsor, the finance director. He would regularly receive a list of complaints about us and call in John to discuss them. John would go through them and almost invariably find that none of them had been raised with him by his project manager. The implications of this were that the client staff were breaking the agreement with us, where issues should be raised through the project structure, and were simply sending secret complaints to the sponsor direct.

Fortunately the sponsor's view of this was the right one – he refused to accept any complaints unless it could be shown that they had come through the agreed channels, and this eliminated almost all of them. Because of him, the project did reach a conclusion, based on the terms of engagement we had renegotiated.

This is the kind of client you might want to avoid completely, if you can detect the culture problems early enough in the sales process. Often this is not possible, in which case identifying the political structure and building a really solid relationship with the project sponsor is vital. Without this, the project would have been impossible to complete.

When the client demonstrated lack of commitment early on, a renegotiation of contract terms was absolutely the right thing to do. To soldier on would have given the client scope to blame you, as things went further off track.

Having a really tight complaints procedure, agreed up front with the client, was also vital in this situation. In fact, all operating procedures, especially change control, need to be dealt with in the same clear and firm way.

Progress now

- Think about the client(s) you currently work with.
- Can you describe their political structure?
- Do you know your allies and your opponents?
- How well do you brief your manager on client politics?

CHAPTER 14

Influencing and Negotiation

You have not converted a man because you have silenced him.

JOHN MORLEY

Use soft words and hard arguments.

ENGLISH PROVERB

ELEMENTS OF INFLUENCE

Sitting at the core of influencing skills is a critical value which underlies all relationships – **trust**. Without trust, influencing skills will not work: **no trust = no influence**.

People see the application of influencing skills without trust as manipulation, and react accordingly. If you are thinking this is obvious, can you honestly say that you have never tried to influence someone without having established trust and then discovered that it does not work?

When I asked Leon Sadler from SAP UK Ltd about building client relationships, he said: 'I endeavour to create opportunities and give them reasons to trust me.' Clearly this is not something you do to the client – they choose whether to trust you or not.

Learning all the persuasive words in the book will not win you influence, unless for a short while at least, you have also won trust. 'Would you buy a used car from this man?' is a well-worn cliché, but is another way of saying 'Do you trust him?'

Why should the client trust you? Trust is normally built over time: you keep your promises; what you say is seen to be accurate and truthful; you are open about what you do, what you know, and also what you do not know.

In addition to this objective verification, people also detect **nonverbal signals**, which they associate – not always correctly – with trustworthy people. These include the classics, like looking people in the eye, sounding confident and relating strongly to the other person's needs. The unscrupulous used car salesman succeeds largely through doing this well. They also have qualities of apparent openness and might appear to confess to something minor, in order to build a reputation of honesty.

This can all be summarized as building rapport, which was covered in Chapter 12. To influence successfully:

- Build rapport
- Act with integrity
- Value the other person's interests

Jodi and Carol have been working together on a project for only a short while, and Jodi's performance is erratic. They are consequently a little behind schedule and Jodi suggests working over the weekend to catch up.

'We don't need to do that, Jodi. If we just work a bit longer early next week, we can soon catch up. The review meeting isn't till Thursday, so we've plenty of time.'

'I'd feel more comfortable if we were back on track by Monday, Carol. We could do it if we just worked Saturday and Sunday morning.'

'I really don't want to do that – I've got a lot on this weekend, and it would be difficult to fit in the time. I really don't see why . . .'

'Carol, you're really efficient, I'm sure you could manage at least a long half day.'

You can see that Jodi is not getting anywhere with her attempts at persuasion. There are several reasons for this.

1   Carol has found Jodi's work to be erratic, therefore she questions her reliability.

2   Jodi's commitment is also in question, for the same reason, and this desire to work at the weekend is therefore inconsistent with her previous behaviour.

3   Because of this, Carol may suspect an ulterior motive, which
    Jodi is not telling her about.

4   Jodi has not given Carol sufficient motive to work at the
    weekend, and indeed is not sensitive to Carol's needs in this
    regard.

All this adds up to the fact that Carol does not trust Jodi, and
does not feel that Jodi has Carol's interest at heart. Carol decides
to play it straight with Jodi:

'Look, Jodi, you've said nothing to convince me to do this. Let's
be completely open about things – tell me the real reason why
you want to work at the weekend?'

After some hesitation, Jodi explains that she is having problems
with her partner, which is why her performance has been
erratic. He is away on business over the weekend, but they have
agreed to spend plenty of time together next week to sort things
out.

'So tell me what's in it for me, Jodi?'

'Not a lot, I suppose, Carol, now I think about it, except some
free time next week when you don't need it. I think if I work for
longer at the weekend, I can probably cover for both of us, so you
can forget the whole thing, and perhaps just do a little checking

on Monday. I'm sorry I raised the issue at all – you just enjoy your weekend.'

Do you think that Carol will go along with Jodi's last suggestion? In reality, she decides differently:

'Well, Jodi, now I understand the real situation, I'll be happy to help. I'll come in for a couple of hours on Saturday morning, we can divide up the work, and then I'll carry on again on Monday, and if necessary Tuesday evenings – that should cover all eventualities, and leave me free to enjoy most of my weekend.'

Several things have happened to enable this change to take place.

1 Jodi has been open about her problems and her motive.

2 She has satisfactorily explained her erratic behaviour.

3 Both of these things allow Carol to trust her to a reasonable degree.

4 Jodi has recognized, with some prompting, that she is not offering any incentive to Carol and has therefore withdrawn her request for help.

This has the immediate effect of removing the pressure from Carol. This is a critical step in the influencing process: giving people the freedom not to do what you are suggesting. When this happens, Carol decides that she will help after all, on her terms and under no pressure, with the motive of helping out someone with a problem she understands and can identify with.

Key messages

- 🕊 Honesty leads to trust
- 🕊 Seeing the other person's perspective is vital
- 🕊 Removing the pressure is a powerful tool

Even when you have good rapport and trust in a long-standing relationship, influencing can still be a challenge.

Jason has been working with Nigel for many months and they get on well together. Jason wants to introduce some new software into the project, but Nigel is resisting.

'We don't need it, Jay. By the time we've both got the hang of it, we'll have wasted more time than we've saved.'

'But Don tells me that it will have a real impact. He's been raving about it ever since he tried it.'

'I don't have a lot of faith in what Don says. Let's just carry on as we are.'

Jason is clearly not getting anywhere with Nigel. He has rapport, and mutual trust. He's offered Nigel a good reason to change, but he won't accept it. At this point, Jason asks a critical and much neglected question. It is much neglected because it is so obvious, and because it is so obvious, people feel that they should not ask it, that they need to be more subtle.

'What do I have to do to convince you about this software, Nigel?'

'I'm not sure you can do anything, Jay.'

'Is there nothing that would persuade you?'

'Can't think of anything.'

'Do you want to be persuaded?'

'No, not really.'

'And why's that?'

'I don't want to have anything to do with anything that Don has recommended. He thinks he knows it all and I just don't want to give him the satisfaction of using the stuff.'

Now Jason knows what he's up against. If he had continued with his original line of persuasion, it would have led nowhere. Instead he asked those two vital questions:

🐾 'What do I have to do to convince to/persuade you to . . . ?'

🐾 'Do you want to be persuaded?'

Not everyone will give you the answer on a plate, but some will. Most will give you some useful information and you have little to lose by asking. If you think that the question is unsubtle and will make your intentions plain, you are probably labouring under the false illusion that your intentions are hidden. Most people on the receiving end of any persuasive approach are normally only too aware of what is going on, and will almost be relieved to receive an open question.

Progress now

- Find a non-critical opportunity to practise your influencing skills.

- Build rapport so that you feel in tune with the other person, have matched and paced them, and can lead them in the direction you want them to go.

- Act with integrity so that trust is established as early as possible. Above all, this means being open and delivering whatever you commit to deliver.

- See the other person's viewpoint and identify what is in it for them.

- Ask how best to convince them.

- Demonstrate how you can meet their needs and if you can enable them to discover that for themselves, so much the better.

- Take the pressure off so that they feel they have choice and can make their own decision. This is the most powerful form of persuasion.

THE WIN–WIN APPROACH TO NEGOTIATION

First consider when you will need negotiation skills. As a consultant, you will encounter the need to negotiate in various situations, no matter what role you play. You may be involved in the sales process, where negotiation is almost always a key element. You may only get involved post-sales, when everything is supposedly nailed down tightly, but invariably the customer will ask for something that is not in the specification or will want to bring forward a date or make some change to methodology, which will mean that you end up negotiating with them. This means that wherever you are in the consulting field, you will need negotiation skills.

Your mind-set

Your mental approach to negotiation is all. If you hold the presupposition that there is a solution to every problem, this will help to deliver the key skill you need for negotiation: **creativity** – the creativity to find that solution and to create a **win-win outcome**.

The win-win outcome sounds like a cliché, but only because it works! This will also be part of your mind-set – you are not seeking victory at your client's expense. You are creatively searching for that solution which delivers victory to you both and is the best way to meet both your needs. A key message is not to take what the client wants at face value, but to find the real need.

SB Engineering

The small engineering company that Judy works for has never used a consultant before. It feels like a great extravagance to most of them, and Judy's time and effort have been monitored closely. It is only a small project, to produce an outline salary structure, and Judy is progressing well when Peter, the MD, makes a casual remark which throws her completely.

'Will we need to invest in new hardware for the system you are proposing?'

She is uncertain how to respond but decides to take the bull by the horns there and then.

'I think you may have misunderstood what I am delivering at the end of next week. A new salary system is the structure you will use; I am not looking at the software to administer it.'

'But that's what we're expecting.'

'I didn't know that until this moment! It's not in the brief though, and I would not expect to . . .'

'What do you mean, not in the brief! It says a new salary system, and that's what we're paying you for!'

How do you think Judy is feeling now? You, sitting calmly

observing, are in the best position to tell her that she now has a negotiation opportunity to enjoy. That she will need to be feeling at her most creative at this moment and wanting to make the client feel good by generating a win-win outcome.

Since you know very well that she is feeling none of these things right now, you can readily identify with the difficulty of doing a brilliant piece of negotiation on the spot, from the back foot. So what is your advice to Judy?

Get off the hot spot and off the back foot. Buy some time for you both to calm down and for you to get creative. Feel an equal power balance between you and the client, so that you can be assertive but never aggressive. Keep emotion out of any negotiation, no matter how provoking the client may be.

Judy does as you advise:

'Peter, I can see that we have a major issue here. Let me go away and think about it for a little while, then I'll come and see you to discuss it. When are you free this afternoon?'

'Any time after three. The sooner the better – but can't we deal with it now? I'm very unhappy about this.'

'That makes two of us, Peter, but I need some time to put some thoughts together. I'll see you at three.'

In buying this time, Judy has been careful not to diminish the problem. Peter knows that it is a major issue and totally unsolved at this point. She has not made any reassuring noises because she does not have a solution at this moment, but she now has time to think and get herself into the positive and creative frame of mind she needs to find the solution that she knows is there for her win–win outcome.

The one question that you might want to ask her now is whether she has enough information about the client's expectations to find her solution. If not, she needs to get as much as possible now, before she starts working on the problem. At present, she has defined the problem as:

'Client expects recommendations for software as well as new salary system. I have not quoted to do this, and do not have time to do it by Friday. Client will not pay any extra for it.'

The definition is flawed, in that the last item is an assumption on her part, although in the context of their penny-pinching approach to the whole project, it is a pretty reasonable assumption. So the solution she sets about finding is one that enables her to offer a system recommendation, at no extra cost to the client, without her having to give more time free of charge.

At her meeting with Peter she first of all tests her definition:

'Peter, can we start with cards on the table. Tell me exactly what you are expecting from me on Friday.'

Peter confirms what she suspects.

'Now, from my side, Peter, I quoted for a new system, meaning a document covering the new structure. I saw the choice of software as a next step, requiring more work from me, if you chose to commission me to do it.'

Peter reconfirms that the company will not pay any more and indeed will feel cheated by her price if it excludes this key element.

'So we need to find a way of delivering this extra piece, without any further costs to you or me?'

'If you want to put it like that. Your costs and time are your affair. I just want what I believe I'm paying for.'

Although the client will often push aside your needs, it is important to establish them clearly, as Judy has done here, so that they become a significant part of the negotiation even if the client does not acknowledge this point overtly.

'My proposal is this, Peter. I can recommend an excellent software company that I have worked with before. I can't be sure that they will have an exact fit with your requirements, but they are very flexible and reasonably priced. I therefore suggest that we invite them in now, and arrange for them to work with me during the latter part of next week. As my work is completed, they will be able to put together a proposal in parallel. You will then have your system and your software recommendation on Friday, at no extra cost.'

'Suppose we don't like their quote and go somewhere else?'

'That's your decision. I doubt that they would make a charge for producing a proposal, so you would still have no additional costs.'

'Then we'd be on our own. You wouldn't help us to choose another vendor, would you?'

'Not unless you had a very serious reason for rejecting the company I propose. But I'm sure you won't.'

'Give me some information now. I'd like to know more about them.'

Peter will not give Judy the satisfaction of openly accepting the deal, but this last remark tells Judy that, provided her software company plays ball, she has her win-win outcome.

You can draw a number of key messages from Judy's experience:

1 She used time well, deferring the negotiation until she could get into the right frame of mind. The client was impatient but she did not give in.

2 She checked the problem definition with the client, to ensure that she was looking for the right solution.

3 She was confident of finding a solution and making it a win-win one.

4 She was assertive and clear about what she needed to make it a win for her.

5 She did not behave as if the client had all the power.

THE OTHER PARTY'S INTERESTS

Sometimes the client does not recognize that what they ask for is not what they really need. This search can be applied just as effectively to a seemingly obvious negotiation item, like price. A client may say they want a cheap option, but it may be that *when* they pay is more important than *what* they pay. It may be that they need to be seen to be getting a huge discount and the starting price is therefore less important than the percentage cut they 'negotiate' from you. The key skill is to put yourself in the client's place, and see the situation through their eyes.

There are two stages in doing this. The first is to sit where the client sits and say to yourself: 'If I were the client, what would I want?'

The second stage is to sit where the client sits and say to yourself: 'If I were this client, this person, with a different set of values and priorities from me, what would this person want?'

The two are quite different. Getting into the second position is more of a challenge, since you need to know a lot about the client. The more you know, the better you will be able to understand what they want of you.

SAP

This case study on negotiation comes from Leon Sadler at SAP, who told me that it was one of the most difficult client situations he has had to face.

'We were working for a medium-sized client in the communications industry and they had contracted a project manager to run the whole implementation, since they had no expertise themselves. Sadly, we rapidly discovered that the project manager, John, was not very skilled and he started to create major problems. I sat down with him and tried to build a relationship, saying that if we didn't work together, it would reflect badly on both of us. John was too insecure to accept this and went back to the client and complained about us. This problem went on for some time and we tried to work around it, but in the end I had to go to the sponsor and tell all.

The sponsor was horrified.

'Leon, are you telling me the man's incompetent?'

'Sam, I really didn't want to do this, but I've tried everything and it just isn't working.' I gave Sam real evidence of the problem, which he had to accept.

'Leon, if I sack John now, then I will look incompetent too and the board would eat me for breakfast. I've practically staked my career on this project.'

'I could bring in my own project manager, but that would involve significant extra cost . . .'

'I can't possibly extend the budget, Leon. If I ask for more money, they'll want to know why and we're back with the same problem. You'll just have to work with John as best you can.'

'Believe me, Sam, I've tried. I wouldn't be sitting here now if I could make it work. Unless you're prepared for a minimum four-week delay on the project, something's got to give.'

'We can't be even a day late!'

'I know, Sam. Leave it with me for a while, I won't leave you exposed.'

Leon takes time to think about the problem. He is very clear on the client's needs, and understands why he cannot manoeuvre on price or timing or on the contractor. This makes a win–win outcome very hard to achieve, if he defines it as meeting the client's needs, at no extra to cost to SAP.

Leon chose to define win–win differently. He would meet the client's needs, and preserve his company's reputation. He agreed with Sam to move the contractor to manage a smaller part of the project, where he had appropriate skills. Leon then brought in his own project manager, at his cost, to complete the project on time.

'I made no profit, but the project was a great success, the contractor co-operated in his new role, and the client was very happy indeed.'

Clearly, Leon made a major concession here, but he won on all other counts, even keeping the contractor on side, and he did not make a loss, so he was happy to consider this a win-win for SAP.

It is not a perfect world – we do not always get what we want, so be very clear about your priorities in a negotiation. Leon's were:

1 Reputation of SAP – linked with
2 Successful project.
3 Profit target.

When he had explored all avenues, and seen that he could not achieve all three, Leon was very clear about which one he could be flexible on. He may regain that lost profit, either from new business earned on the basis of that success, or from the deeply grateful project sponsor, when he moves to another company.

Progress now

When faced with a potential negotiation, remember the presupposition: 'The person with the most flexibility in thinking and behaviour has the most influence on any interaction. Overt exercise of power, unless taken to extremes, will not win the battle against the flexible thinker'.

🔄 Start by understanding what the client really wants.

🔄 Do not be pressured into negotiating before you are ready.

🔄 Take time out to think and get into the right mind-set.

🔄 Think positively, believing that there is a solution to every problem.

🔄 Feel an even balance of power between you and the client.

🔄 Be very clear about your priorities in the negotiation.

🔄 Make your needs clear to the client, so that they feel the balance of the negotiation.

🔄 Remain assertive throughout – persevering and unemotional.

🔄 Get into the client's head and see things from their perspective.

🔄 Look for as many variables as possible and be creative.

🔄 Find the win-win solution you know is there.

CHAPTER 15

Dealing with Internal Relationships

You get the best out of others when you give the best of yourself.

HARRY FIRESTONE

No man is wise enough by himself.

TITUS MACCIUS PLAUTUS (254–184 BC),
Miles Gloriosus

🔊 **Working alone on site**
🔊 **Working in a team**
🔊 **Working with other contractors**

WORKING ALONE ON SITE

If you are working alone on a customer site for several months or more, a number of things may happen to you, quite apart from those related to the project you are working on. The consequences have rather more implications if you are an employee than if you work for yourself.

There are three major issues:

1　A sense of becoming cut off from your company

2　A feeling of divided loyalties

3　A feeling of belonging to the client, otherwise known as 'going native'

You might think that the three are a progression, which they could be, but it is possible to suffer (or enjoy!) any one of them.

The victim

Susan has been working alone on site for four months, and it is driving her mad. She is in an office on her own with no windows and poor light; the client staff are friendly but really busy, and have little time to socialize. It is also the type of work that she has done several times before and, despite her requests for broader experience, she always seems to end up doing the same thing. She has asked to go on a training course, but nothing has happened.

When she sees her manager, Helen, there is only time to talk about the project and then Helen is off to her next meeting. Susan sends Helen an e-mail, requesting the training, but she has not replied.

If you were Susan, what would you do now?

- You could pick up the newspaper and start job hunting.

- You could complain to human resources (HR).

- You could demand time with your manager to discuss these issues.

- You could soldier on and hope for the best.

It would be easy to go down a negative route at this point – either by complaining or leaving. However, it can be very effective to simply take the initiative and see what happens.

Susan goes to see the client and asks if she can move to a different working area. After a week, this is arranged without difficulty.

Susan writes an e-mail to her manager, telling her that she will be making a booking for the training course, which will take place in two months' time. She then rings the HR department, makes the booking, and asks them to organize the sign-off procedure with her boss, as she is out on site all the time.

She then rings her boss's secretary and asks her to block out two hours for her next site visit, not one, as she wants a personal discussion. She e-mails her manager to confirm this. When that meeting does eventually take place, her manager is a little taken aback at the things that Susan has done, but can hardly complain that she was not informed about them, and ends up by applauding the proactive stance that Susan has taken. This is Susan's cue to extract a promise that, after her training, she can work on a different type of project, to which her manager readily agrees.

Progress now

◊ Recognize when you are in danger of going native and decide where your loyalties lie.

◊ If you have been 'disloyal' and still want to work for your employer, take proactive steps to rebuild the relationship.

◊ If you feel neglected and in 'victim' mode, take the initiative and make something happen, while keeping your manager informed.

◊ Make a formal request for some of your manager's time for a personal discussion, if necessary.

◊ Take responsibility for implementing your own training and development plan.

WORKING IN A TEAM

As a consultant, you will probably find yourself working frequently in a project team. By their very nature, they tend to form quickly for relatively short periods, so there is little time for the 'forming, storming and norming', which is the natural process that many teams go through on their way to stability and effectiveness.

If you set about your role as a team member in a proactive way, you can make a significant contribution to the process of building a team quickly, and help the team leader rather than leaving all the responsibility to them, as many team members do.

As a good team player, you will be:

- A good communicator who listens, informs and asks for information
- Open and honest
- Nice to people, but not afraid to deal with conflict if it arises
- Helpful to other team members, looking out for them and not purely focused on your own role

- ▷ Loyal to the team
- ▷ Positive, with a sense of humour

In this context, it is helpful to hold two presuppositions: '*The map is not the territory*' and '*the meaning of communication is in the response you get*'. These two will focus your thinking on the views of other people and their 'map' or view of the world, and on the fact that what people hear is often not what left your lips!

As a good team member, aiding the communication process is one of the most important roles you can perform, especially in team meetings when you can ask questions for clarification or to encourage someone to speak when you know they have something to say. Teams rarely fail because of over-communication, but things often go wrong for the opposite reason.

Communication

An extreme example of communication difficulties was given by David Mitchell of Oracle UK Ltd, who was sent out to an eastern bloc country to retrieve a public utilities project, which was slipping six weeks every month.

'For the project to slip at this rate was quite an achievement and it proved a real challenge. I was the only English-speaking person there and I was assigned a full-time interpreter. It was the middle of winter, very cold, with no heating in the main office, and the canteen's very best effort was tripe and beetroot, both of which I hate!'

'When I got there, I discovered the problem was that no one could make a decision. In the post-communist world, where previously the State had decided everything, no one had any idea how to make a decision or, more importantly, how to take responsibility for it. I analysed the situation from the top to the bottom of the organization and it was the same throughout. However, the people at the top did say that they were happy for the people at the bottom to make decisions, to which the people lower down immediately asked: 'Which ones can we make?'

'To break this mould, I spent time coaching the team and the project managers in making decisions and, more important than that, encouraging them to make mistakes and see that the consequences were not fatal. I decided that working from the bottom up would be most effective, and so it proved. The major challenge was that all this had to be done through an interpreter, but I succeeded and put the project back on track to a successful conclusion. It was very rewarding to help to empower people and to see them respond to this new-found freedom.'

You may think that this is a problem generated by communist rule but fear of making decisions can hold a team back in any political culture – even the most democratic.

Openness and honesty

Being open with people is the fastest way to build trust, and trust is the foundation of an effective team. When the information is yours, then share it – be it good news or bad. If there is a problem, you are giving others the opportunity to help you to solve it. If that makes you feel exposed in front of the rest of the team, then console yourself with the fact that they are valuing your open and honest approach.

Being positive and supportive

Have you ever been in one of those project meetings where someone always takes the negative view? They think that they are pointing out difficulties in a constructive manner, but the message that leaves them is not the one that the rest of the group hears.

'Well, I think we should stop and review the whole thing.'

'Simon, that would put the project back at least a week.'

'But this is a serious problem. If it goes the way I predict, then we're on the road to complete disaster.'

The rest of the team now argue with Simon and tell him he is being a pessimist and overreacting. Simon gets upset. The team leader overrules his objections and the meeting ends on a sour note.

If Simon had framed his issue in a positive way, he might have had a different response.

'Now look, folks, I know you're going to hate me for raising this, but I've found what could be a serious problem.'

'Not again, Simon!'

'I'm afraid so. Now I don't want this to cause a project delay, so can we examine this together and see if we can solve it here?'

At this point Simon gets murmurs of assent and he is off on a positive track, taking the team with him.

In addition to a positive approach, active support for other team members really helps to build a team fast. This can mean any number of things: paying a compliment in public or in private; helping someone with a problem; supporting someone's contribution to a meeting. A simple practical way to oil the wheels of a team is to resolve to say something nice to someone every day – and mean it!

Progress now

- ❧ Take active responsibility for helping the team to work well together.
- ❧ Communicate to clarify, inform and to help other team members do the same.
- ❧ Be open and honest.
- ❧ Deal openly with conflict if it arises.
- ❧ Oil the team wheels with good humour and positive remarks.
- ❧ Be loyal and supportive to the team.

WORKING WITH OTHER CONTRACTORS

When you are working on larger projects, you will often find that you are working with other suppliers in various ways. You may be the prime contractor or you may be one of a number of small subcontractors. You may have been chosen by the client or by the prime contractor.

Each of these scenarios can present operating problems, not necessarily because of the nature of the other suppliers, but because of the complexity of a three-tier relationship. There is plenty of scope for communication problems to arise. The key is to recognize the situation and anticipate as much as possible. As prime contractor, you will obviously take responsibility for agreeing objectives and managing the progress and quality of the work of other suppliers but, as a subcontractor, it is in your interest to make sure that this is done well and not to just take a passive role. Whatever your relationship, spend as much, if not more, time on setting up the project parameters with other suppliers as you would with the client – this is the best way to avoid problems.

Disagreement between suppliers

However, no amount of agreement of objectives and project milestone reviews will solve political problems. Understanding the politics, and finding a way around them or above them is the key.

Problems can arise when suppliers disagree over something major. Helen and Nigel just cannot agree on a project milestone, 24 hours before the client review meeting.

'We're there, Nigel! No need for all this extra work you're proposing . . .'

'Sorry Helen, I just don't agree and, as it's ultimately my company's responsibility, I'm going to have to tell the client there will be a week's delay.'

'I can't support that. You are wasting time.'

'We must present a united front to the client.'

'Not when it wrongly shows my company in a bad light!'

'It won't look too good if we can't agree, though will it?'

'But I really believe I'm right and we're not running late, and I want the client to know that.'

'They'll end up doing what I recommend, as prime contractor.'

'That's as maybe, but at least I'll have put my case.'

Nigel positions the topic very carefully at the client meeting the next day.

'Helen and I have discussed this point at length, and have agreed to disagree. Helen believes that we have reached the milestone. I do not. I strongly recommend that we take another week to do this. Would you like us to debate this with you or will you accept my recommendation?'

This is the best form of damage limitation that Nigel can achieve. He has maintained a clear position of control and has avoided an argument in front of the client. If the client asks for a debate it will be a measured presentation of views with no antagonism. Nothing upsets a client more than being faced by squabbling contractors offering conflicting advice.

An extension of this problem is where suppliers not only disagree, but start blaming each other.

As an example, Helen might have blurted out in the meeting:

'I don't agree with Nigel because in not agreeing to the milestone, he is implicitly blaming my team for their work. That is a completely unfounded criticism and I can prove it to you!'

Now the client is being asked to arbitrate between the two of them and the client hates being put in this position; think of their perspective before you leap to the defence of your company.

Ultimately, supplier relationships are about mutual benefit, loyalty and trust. If you approach your fellow suppliers in an open and positive manner, while holding those values, you will go a long way to achieving all that mutual benefit.

Progress now

- Understand the nature of your supplier relationships in any project.
- Take care to clarify all the project parameters with them.
- Present a united front to the client.
- Aim for openness, loyalty and trust as your prime values in any supplier relationship. If you start from there, with positive expectations, you are more likely to get positive responses in return.

CHAPTER 16
Marketing Your Services

We aim above the mark to hit the mark.

RALPH WALDO EMERSON

Only those who dare to fail greatly can ever achieve greatly.

ROBERT FRANCIS KENNEDY

- 🞧 **What are you selling?**
- 🞧 **The lure of the brochure**
- 🞧 **Review of marketing tools**

WHAT ARE YOU SELLING?

From the very start of this book we have been clear that people buy integrity, reliability and credibility before they buy technical expertise from a consultant. Integrity and reliability cannot be easily sold. If they are thrust at a client, they are likely to reject them, and this is the intrinsic difficulty in marketing consulting services using any of the traditional methods, such as advertising or mailings. You can promote your technical expertise and, if that is sufficiently rare, people will respond. Unfortunately few of us are offering such a rare commodity and the client's key to choosing between all the competitive technical offerings is to find ways to test their need for integrity and reliability.

The most obvious route is to seek recommendations from friends or colleagues – people whose opinion they trust. Failing that, they will look at track record and ask to speak to previous clients.

What they are almost certainly not buying is a services product. They want to know that you have experience in, for example, setting up call centres. They do not want your standard formula for doing so because their call centre is going to be different. Bear this in mind if you decide you need a brochure: the essence of what you can 'sell' in a brochure is your professionalism (often conveyed by the physical elements of the brochure itself), your technical expertise, your flexibility to meet differing client needs, and your track record of success. If a client senses that they are going to be straitjacketed into your standard solution, this will be a great turn off for them.

THE LURE OF THE BROCHURE

For consulting services, a brochure will never be a major element in the sales process, but it can detract from it if not well done. At best, it plays a professional but relatively small supporting role. If you are just starting up as a consultant, do not go down the brochure route – you will be wasting your not-yet-earned money at this stage! Vic Hartley of Vertex Consultants gives some real pearls of wisdom on this subject:

'It is important to be really clear about what you are providing to the market place. I created a brochure of my services and I got the names of managing directors of the companies I was targeting. So I sent out 200 personal letters with my brochure and I got one reply! It's so obvious to me now that that's what will happen; so my advice is to design a brochure to be clear in your mind what you want to offer and then throw it away! Having a focus, that's the important thing. I might use a brochure after I have held a first meeting with a prospect but, otherwise, they are not useful. Indeed you could say that, since you are offering a tailored service to meet the client's needs, then it's not congruent to offer them a brochure. You cannot sell a tailored service with a standardized mailing.

'At the same time as designing a brochure, I listed 17 names of people to approach, just contacts on a scrap of paper. I followed them up and out of 17 names I got work from 11, whereas my mailing of 200 had produced one lead and no work! Service is about talking to people and selling yourself. You need contacts to get to know people and move outwards from there.'

Mary Ahmad from Corporate HR Partners has a similar story: 'I went through the stage of writing lots of marketing letters, which I think everybody does, but nothing much comes of them and then I moved on to networking opportunities – things like the IOD, the American Chamber of Commerce, etc.'

The message of experience is consistent – successful marketing of consulting services is about networking, contacts and referrals.

Someone who has taken another successful route is Peter Honey of Peter Honey Learning, who keeps a very high profile through his writing. Not only is he a well-known author, but he appears regularly in professional magazines which, in addition to profile raising, enhance his credibility and reinforce his technical expertise. Since this is laid out so openly for public inspection, it provides a big step towards establishing integrity.

REVIEW OF MARKETING TOOLS

Here is a checklist of each of the marketing elements with commentary on their appropriateness for marketing consulting skills.

Advertising

Often expensive. Not an effective medium for the personal message you need to convey. Good if you have a special skill or a unique offering and/or a tightly targeted audience. For example, if you are the only mobile computer expert in your area, it is a good idea to advertise in the local newspaper or parish magazines. Your expertise is not unique, but your location and mobility are, and your audience is tightly targeted and inexpensive to reach.

On the other hand, if you are a management consultant specializing in appraisal systems, unless you have a narrow focus – for example, you cover the bee-keeping market, where there are specialist magazines – advertising will do nothing for you.

Public Relations (PR)

Writing 'technical' articles for relevant magazines can be a very effective marketing exercise, as evidenced by Peter Honey. Getting any kind of positive press coverage is good, although do not waste your time trying to woo journalists unless you know you have something really interesting for them to write about.

PR also covers sponsorship and corporate entertainment. Sponsorship is normally about raising the profile of your company and is a very indirect route, if indeed a route at all, to increasing sales. Corporate entertainment can be useful, as it comes under the heading of making contacts and direct contact with prospects is the only sure way to create a sale.

Direct mail

Not appropriate, as described previously.

Telesales

Could be used to get appointments for a first contact, otherwise inappropriate.

Exhibitions

Inappropriate unless you are targeting those bee-keepers again!

Seminars

Another means of generating contacts and therefore useful if you have the funds to set them up. Offer real content and make it clear that this is not a sales pitch in disguise. Work on an acceptance rate of one in ten even with warm, rather than cold, contacts. Send a written invitation and then do all the follow up on the telephone. For small organizations, all this hard work may not pay off and it may be better to put the same effort into setting up individual meetings.

Networking

This is a vital marketing activity and falls into two areas. First, use all your personal contacts and then all their contacts. To quote Mary Ahmad again: 'The advice is to contact everyone you know, so I would ask them all, "If you were me, who would you be talking to?" I said this to avoid asking them the question directly. The good thing is that your contacts tend to move around between jobs and spread the word around.'

The second form of networking is via organized groups such as the Institute of Directors or any of the myriad of local meetings set up by the local Chamber of Commerce or the local group of

IT companies, etc. If you are working alone or as a very small business, these groups can be an invaluable source of contacts and leads, but possibly also of colleagues you may wish to collaborate with or use as a sounding board.

In addition to these business groups, there are also specific organizations for consultants, such as the IMC, or Magenta Circle, as well as for specialist consulting groups, such as the British Computer Society.

Intermediaries

Everyone is familiar with the contract agency which has served the IT industry in particular for a long time. The recent changes in tax legislation have made this market less attractive, but these agencies remain a useful source of work for many independent consultants.

The internet has produced a new breed of intermediary who operate quite differently and provide a virtual market place for consultants. You pay a small annual fee as a consultant to belong to the service and the employer pays a bigger fee on hiring. You provide your details to the service and the employers provide details of their opportunities. You then negotiate directly, with no other fees involved.

Examples of organizations that provide this service are Magenta Circle and Skillfair (details in the references section). As this is a young and dynamic market place, it is likely that new organizations will have appeared by the time you read this book; try an internet search for consulting agencies and see what you find.

Your daily marketing activity

In reality, the best marketing you can do is to market yourself really well to your current client by doing and being seen to do an excellent job. Towards the end of a project you might ask them for leads. Do they know of anyone who might need your services – now or in the future? As you carefully cultivate each client, they will become a source of repeat or referral business, and this is marketing at its very best.

SUMMARY

1   Marketing consulting services needs to involve personal contact to be effective.

2   If you are small, focus on contacts, networking and intermediaries.

3   If you are larger, enhance contacts and networking with seminars and PR activities.

CHAPTER 17

Starting and Running Your Own Business

The whole world steps aside for the man who knows where he is going.

ANON

Luck is good learning meeting opportunity.

IAN CUNNINGHAM

THREE SUCCESS STORIES

For those of you who are about to set up your own business, or are planning to do so in the future, this chapter contains advice on the basics, and also the experience of three very different consultants, who have made a success of setting up on their own.

PETER HONEY

Peter Honey Learning

After graduation, Peter Honey did four jobs for two major companies: Ford and British Airways. He then decided that a couple of years as a consultant would give him breadth of experience. Those two years turned into a working lifetime, during which there has been only one summer when he has had nothing in the pipeline. Asked about his obvious success in building a business, he replied: 'I was never conscious of doing any marketing.' However, if you consider that Peter has written over 20 books and 100 articles, and has a worldwide reputation for his work on learning styles, you will understand a key attribute of his success.

PH: In the early days I depended on word of mouth and referrals. I'm cynical about respect for the published word – I've written because I love it.

There are consultants who are truly learned experts. I believe in being a learning consultant. I have a low opinion of management consultants who dish out answers. Diagnosis is so vital – it's more than half the job. I work with a client, I'm not an expert on a pedestal and I don't have ready-made answers. With many clients it's a learning together relationship. I tell them that there is no need for me to know everything that they know, otherwise they will have spoiled the distinctive competence I bring – a fresh approach.

My advice is to do a real job first, to learn the fundamentals of the world of work and particularly to understand the politics, before you become a consultant.

MARY AHMAD

Corporate HR Partners

Mary Ahmad started her own business from a very different point in her career. She says:

Once you get to be an HR Director, you don't do much HR. You spend your time managing managers and the relationship with the parent company.

One day I was talking to a multinational about a job they had, and because they had different departments in different locations they wanted an HR person to integrate them. They had several marketing departments for different parts of the company and I said that I expected that would create a lot of problems and they said it did, and suddenly I could see it all and I realized that I didn't want to do this any more. I didn't want any more of the politics – I can do the politics, but I didn't want to – I just didn't have another corporate in me. I was 48.

I had always said that I didn't want to be in corporate life after 50, so I took some time and I thought about what I might do. I realized, after some fanciful ideas, that people would pay me for what I know. My brother-in-law is a consultant and I didn't want to appear to be a one-woman band, working from home, so I shared his office. That meant I had someone to speak to, which was important on the days when I didn't feel motivated. My brother-in-law's business was called Corporate Venture Partners Ltd, so I called myself Corporate HR Partners. So I had an office and a name, now I needed to develop a business.

I started in 1995. At the beginning of 1998 my fellow Director, Andrew, joined and that made a significant difference. We now have clients on retained services and a more complete HR offering. It took off more. We have never been there to carve out a major consulting organization because we want to do the work–home balance thing that is really hard to do when working for a large corporate.

My advice to people setting up on their own is: Find people to talk to – people in similar situations. You need a support network as it can be lonely.

You set off with a business goal and you may well need to modify that because what you think people want and what you discover they want may not be the same thing.

Be careful about your choice of partner in a business. I have a partner who I'd previously worked with for 20 years, who has complementary skills to me, and who I respect and trust. I would never question his integrity and we have a very successful partnership. We did have a third partner, but it did not work as well, not because of lack of trust and respect, far from it, but because our goals and values were different. They were at a different stage in their life and wanted different things. It was amicable, but it did not work because of that and so we parted company.

As a consultant you need confidence and belief in yourself. You have to have broad experience if you are going to set out on your own. You need to become your own IT expert, to buy the stamps and un-jam the photocopiers, in other words to operate at lots of different levels.

VIC HARTLEY

Vertex Consultants

Vic Hartley made very much the same observation as Mary Ahmad. Vic has an interesting background: he has worked for a large consulting group and has set up his own business, and also runs courses on advanced consulting skills. He used to work for Deloittes as Head of Organization Development and Training for the Group. Vic then went on to head up Corporate HR and Management Development for Mercury Communications, which was very much an operational position, before setting up his own business over eight years ago. We asked him first about the transition from a corporate environment to self-employment.

'There was a lot of liberation, but a lot of things I'd taken for granted were not there. In the early stages it was difficult to get to grips with things like computer problems or finance. Not only did this create problems, it also diverted attention from selling and building up the business.

'Another transition difficulty people have is working on their own. They often feel the need to coalesce and maintain some of the structure of corporate life – being together and working together. I dabbled with one or two of these associations, but then I realized that the infrastructure they created was again taking me away from clients. There was also the problem of how to divide up and value any business that was won. It was very difficult to reward all the parties effectively. This can become very difficult and many people have fallen out over it. Every time I see a partnership, I think it must be recent, because generally they don't last.

'I've found that the best way to operate is with a network of peers, which means that I keep my friends. If I sell work and pass it on, I keep a small percentage and they get the rest, and they know that. They do the same with me. Everything is open and up front – everyone recognizes that the sales process has a value and that's fine.

'What this means is that my network overlaps to a small degree with theirs, and then they have their own network and so it goes on. If you trust them, then you can trust anyone they recommend in their network, and so clients also know that they will get people they can trust. The difficulty is in selling the concept that a small company can do as good a job, if not better, than the big names. I know a company in a permanent dilemma because they are very concerned about costs, but always go for the big names. It's a good measure of the confidence and maturity of a client that they are able to employ a small company rather than having to rely on the reputation of a big name. Going for big names often shows that they lack confidence.

(Note: This could be a very neat 'emperor's clothes' pitch to use if you are a small consulting company, selling to a large one, but it needs to be done very carefully!)

'The key skills of a consultant are to listen, keep an open mind and not to go in with a ready-made diagnosis. Recognize that people are different and different does not mean inferior. See things through the client's eyes and help the client to solve the problem, rather than telling the client what to do. If the client loses ownership of a project, then the consultant has to take the blame because that feeling of shared ownership is critical to success. It's also important to acknowledge that the consultant is not always right, just as the customer is not always right, even though you help them to think that they are for much of the time!

'The difference that makes the difference for me is remaining hungry. By hungry I mean that you have the drive and energy to keep the relationships going or to make that phone call or to do the report on time, even though you know they won't look at it for several days. That's what works for me. If I'm just like their own people, then why should they hire me? I've got to be more rigorous, when I hate the detail, more quality aware, more delivery focused.'

Vic's business is about consulting in organization development. 'I help organizations to achieve things that are significant to them, which means I have a very wide portfolio, from designing an appraisal system through to downsizing. I was asked by a client to create a programme for consultants covering advanced consulting skills and that has become a product that I regularly deliver. I did not set out to offer it as part of my portfolio, but it emerged from client needs.'

Progress now

🕭 Setting up on your own will almost certainly be lonely. Get yourself a support network or at least one person who can be your sounding board.

🕭 You need to be a jack-of-all-trades when you start your own business. It will be strategy one minute and sticking on stamps the next.

🕭 Do not waste money on expensive brochures. Write the copy to get clarity of focus on what you are about, but do not print it!

🕭 Use contacts, contacts and more contacts; build your network, both as a source of leads and working associates.

🕭 Do not go into partnership unless your working relationship is tried and tested. If it is, check that your skill sets are truly complementary and finally check that your life values match. For example, long-term versus short-term gain, work–home balance. If you get positives to all these, take some more time and possibly seek some advice, before you decide to take the plunge!

🕭 Start with a clear idea of what your service is and be very prepared to modify it to meet the needs of your clients.

FINANCE, TAX AND LEGAL STATUS

The final part of this chapter deals with a subject which often worries would-be start-ups or, in some cases, does not worry them enough! We can offer you some general advice here, but no specific detail, because personal and business circumstances can differ greatly and legislation changes regularly.

Legal status

A vital question to ask is what your business status should be – whether, for example, you should form a partnership or a limited company. Take tax advice on this, as it will have significant implications for you financially.

Getting advice

The best and cheapest place to start is with the government-sponsored agency designed to help people to set up small businesses. In the UK this is called Business Link and will offer a 'sign-posting' service free of charge. They will help you to decide who you need help from and recommend people to you who are likely to be affordable. Details are in the references section.

Choosing an accountant

Put a great deal of effort into finding the right accountant, before you do almost anything else.

Consider getting some one-off, independent tax advice from a specialist, and then find an accountant to deal with the financial routine. Sometimes you find the two skill sets combined, but often they are not. By consulting an accountant about tax, you may be doing the equivalent of asking your local doctor to do a little brain surgery while you wait.

As a small business, it is possible to do your own accounts and dispense with an accountant. In the same way it is possible to build your own computer or knock up a simple desk to work at. If you have skills in a particular field, by all means use them, and doing your own book-keeping may be sensible. However, if this is not your strength, doing these things is a distraction from your business, not a benefit.

Fees

Setting your fee level can be a challenge. The rule is to do plenty of research and find out what the rates are for your market place.

When you know that, you need to determine where to position yourself – too cheap and people may wonder about the quality of your service; too expensive and they may go elsewhere.

If you decide to vary your rates, be sure to apply a consistent structure. I know some consultants who charge different rates according to the type of work they do and some who charge different rates for different customers – their fees are less to local government, for example. Imagine all your customers in one room, with all the fees they have paid in public view and now explain your pricing structure to them. If you can do this with integrity, your structure is sound.

It can be easier to quote a rate for a complete project, but only if you are very confident of how long it will take. When in doubt, quote fees per day to your client; people have made serious losses on fixed-price contracts.

Tom Lambert has some useful advice on setting fee levels in his book *High Income Consulting* (see the references section for details).

Set-up costs

There is a temptation, when you start on your own, to emulate the major corporations with nice literature, a good business address, all the things that will impress your clients. The joy of setting up as a consultant is that most of the investment is already made – in your head! It also means that clients generally expect you to go to them and not to be invited to your prestigious city centre address.

You will need business cards and possibly letter-headed paper, although you can create your own on your PC. So much correspondence is by e-mail these days that printing stationery may not be worth it.

Office

The question of an office is often down to economics. Unless you offer a service where clients need to visit you, to use specialized equipment, for example, why waste your money? People buy you and your skills; where you keep your PC and your paperwork is not an issue, provided they know you can reach their own offices easily.

Equipment

It goes without saying that you need to be equipped with the tools of your trade, whatever they may be but, if you are a landscape gardener, you do not necessarily need a new PC to write to all your clients – the old one will do.

Sometimes people go into 'new broom' mode with a new business, kitting themselves out with everything new for this fresh start. The result is that you have made a loss before you have even started. Keep your set-up costs to a minimum, ideally just business cards and some advice. Keep asking yourself the same question: will this item bring in more business – and you will be surprised how few things pass this test!

Progress now

🖎 Avail yourself of free information from a government agency.

🖎 Get some one-off tax advice from a specialist at the outset to be clear on your company status.

🖎 Find a business accountant (who is probably not a tax specialist).

🖎 Keep set-up costs to an absolute minimum.

🖎 If you need to spend more on set-up, ask the test question 'Will it bring in more business?' before you make the decision.

CHAPTER 18

Summary

What may be done at any time will be done at
no time.

SCOTTISH PROVERB

What you can do, or dream you can, begin it
now. Boldness has genius, magic and power in
it. Begin it now.

GOETHE

- 🔖 **Act with integrity**
- 🔖 **Listen to your clients**
- 🔖 **Keep learning**

These three messages have occurred most frequently from the interviews and discussions in this book and, although they all sound like pleas to 'be a good consultant' in the ethical sense, do not be fooled. They are the most frequent pieces of advice because they work – they deliver business, repeat business and referrals – the life blood of your future as a consultant.

To reinforce these messages, here they are in context, together with further key points, all in groups of three. You can choose the three which mean the most to you.

As a client, I buy:

- 🔖 Integrity
- 🔖 Reliability
- 🔖 Credibility

before I buy your expertise.

As your prospect, I need you to:

- Really listen to me
- Step into my shoes
- Offer a solution designed just for me

As your client, during a project I need you to:

- Agree with me precisely what you are going to deliver
- Involve me
- Meet my expectations

As a learning consultant, I need:

- Self-belief
- To be ready to fall down one ski run in ten
- To be petrified at least twice a week!

And to help you on your twice weekly ski slope, you will find some useful references in the next section, which is the end of this book, but the beginning of a new journey. Begin it now.

References

GENERAL

E-Learning

The e-learning programme which accompanies this book is called 'The Consultant's Guide to Consulting'. It covers all the key areas of consulting skills and is designed to be interactive with many more case studies, all different from those in the book. Details of the programme can be found at www.avenuemanagement.com.

Learning style

Peter Honey's website is the place to go if you want to find out about your learning style. To complete the Learning Styles Questionnaire online, go to: www.peterhoney.com and click on Learning Styles.

Training/Consulting

Vic Hartley is a partner in Vertex which focuses on advanced skills for consultants and also offers consulting on client management to professional firms. Tel: 00 44 (0)1444 456473.

Q Learning offers many courses which could benefit you as a consultant, as well as personal coaching. In particular, they specialize in areas of outcome thinking and strategies for success, as well as the specifics like project management. Everything you need to take you beyond your best! See www.qlearning.com.

Tom Lambert is known as the consultant's consultant. He has written a number of books on the subject, the most well-known being *High Income Consulting*. www.tom-lambert.com.

Irene Nathan is the Managing Director of the Interpersonal Relations Group and founder President of the Federation of Image Consultants. 'Consultants can volunteer to be a model on a training course for image consultants. They are often looking for people and of course there would be no charge.' The Federation website has details of recognized training providers: www.tfic.org.uk.

PROFESSIONAL BODIES

Whatever your technical field, there will probably be a professional body of some kind offering qualifications. Often these extend to non-technical skills too. A good example is the British Computer Society (BCS). If you are a consultant in the IT field, you may wish to consider the BCS Certificate in Consultancy Practice as a qualification. It covers the broadest spectrum of non-IT subjects, from change management to project risk assessment and details can be found on the BCS website: www.bcs.org.uk.

Apart from specific professional bodies, there are also broader organizations, like the Institute of Management Consultancy (IMC). They also offer a qualification as a Certified Management Consultant, as well as maintaining a register of consultants and various other services: www.imc.co.uk.

FOR SMALL BUSINESS CONSULTANTS

Advice

An obvious starting place for advice on setting up and running your own business is Business Link: 'The national network of advice centres for businesses great and small.' They will always 'know a man who can'. www.businesslink.org.

Networking

The organizations below provide networking opportunities:

Magenta Circle is dedicated to self-employed consultants and does not have the strict attendance rules that can apply to some networks. There are monthly meetings in different locations and the aim is to facilitate networking, both for business opportunities and for mutual support.

Nigel Wyatt, who founded the Circle when he became a consultant, related an interesting fact. As an individual consultant in the financial training arena, he has had more business from competing consultants than from complementary ones: 'They understand exactly what I do and, when they have too much work or a client isn't right for them, they come to me!'

Collaborating with your competitors is an interesting path to follow and other consultants have done so very successfully.

Details of Magenta Circle can be found on their website: www.magentacircle.co.uk.

The best-known and established networking groups are BRE and BNI. They have a long track record in this field and generally work on the basis that you must attend meetings very regularly; they do not normally allow competitors in the same group. However, there are lots of local groups, so this should not be an issue.

BRE is the Business Referral Exchange – www.brenet.co.uk.

BNI is Business Network Inc. – www.bni-europe.com.

Online market place

This area of the Internet is one that is moving fast and well worth exploring if you are an independent consultant.

Here is just one example of the type called Skillfair, which is run by Gill Hunt. Skillfair is an online project exchange for independent consultants in the UK. Clients search for quality checked consultants in Business and IT disciplines or ask Skillfair to find the right person for the project: www.skillfair.co.uk.

Tax

To find out the latest on IR35 or its successor, go to www.inlandrevenue.gov.uk/ir35/.

NOTES

NOTES

NOTES

NOTES

NOTES

Q LEARNING: Consultant